Stellar English

SKILLS FOR SCHOLARS

Stellar English

A Down-to-Earth Guide to Grammar and Style

Frank L. Cioffi

PRINCETON UNIVERSITY PRESS

PRINCETON AND OXFORD

Published by Princeton University Press
41 William Street, Princeton, New Jersey 08540
99 Banbury Road, Oxford OX2 6JX

press.princeton.edu

All Rights Reserved
ISBN 9780691239385
ISBN (pbk.) 9780691239392
ISBN (e-book) 9780691239408

British Library Cataloging-in-Publication Data is available

Editorial: Matt Rohal and Alena Chekanov
Production Editorial: Sara Lerner
Text Design: Carmina Alvarez
Cover Design: Heather Hansen
Production: Erin Suydam
Publicity: Jodi Price and Kathryn Stevens
Copyeditor: Jennifer Harris

This book has been composed in Minion Pro and Futura Std

Printed in the United States of America

1 3 5 7 9 10 8 6 4 2

In memory of my twin brother

Grant Louis Cioffi

(1951–2010)

I am afraid we are not rid of God because
we still have faith in grammar.
—*Friedrich Nietzsche*, Twilight of the Idols, *1895*

Light has no grammar.
—*Robert Macfarlane*, Landmarks, *2015*

Contents

Stellar English

Introduction

Writing matters. You probably agree with this sentiment or might be persuaded to, given that you have picked up this extravagantly titled book and have read its first thirty words.

What am I striving for in this slim volume? I want to guide you toward what I'm calling *stellar English*—an out-of-this-world-effective grammar and usage, something that ChatGPT might only dimly imagine but never replicate in its lifeless, electronic siliconsciousness. You, though, as a living, conscious, sentient entity who recognizes that writing matters—you can attain it.

In order to get you toward stellar English, toward grammatical exactitude and stylistic assurance, this book will present some essentials of formal English: namely, the terms commonly used to describe various parts and aspects of the language, the typical ways that sentences are constructed and punctuated, a small sample of words easily confused, and some cautionary guidelines about major pitfalls to avoid.

I'm not going to claim *Stellar English* will solve your every writing problem. It won't help you navigate the quirks of Microsoft Word, nor will it proofread your writing or protect you from the dreaded "autocorrect." It won't help you meet deadlines. But what it will do, I hope, is increase your mastery of formal English grammar and usage—and simultaneously enhance your credibility and persuasiveness. Now this launch into stellar English won't physically remove you from earth, but language used well can enable your thoughts to soar. A lofty goal? Perhaps. But what's a heaven for?

The Importance of Audience

Here is the key to effective writing. At every stage, from your conception of the initial idea, through fingers-on-keyboard drafting, to the final revision—you always need to keep the following question in mind: Who is your audience? Writing sometimes will veer off like a wild horse that's suddenly decided to bolt crazily ahead; your job is to rein it back in, get it going at the right speed and gait and in the right direction. In your writing, controlling that wild gallop of words involves, to a large extent, figuring out their intended destination. Where are they headed? You have to continually keep this question in mind and adjust your writing accordingly.

Sometimes your audience will be only one reader, which simplifies things. Keeping one person in mind, putting yourself in that reader's place, and seeing your writing through their eyes while focusing on the issue you're writing about is a challenging but manageable task.[1]

---

[1] Note that even though I am talking about only one reader here, I use the plural possessive pronoun "their" [in "their eyes"]. Is that wrong? Some people say it is. I disagree. The "singular they" was once the accepted format (used as early as 1375 [Baron]), then fell into disfavor. It is now the new normal. I will discuss this in greater detail in part 2, pages 94–96.

On the other hand, addressing an audience of more than one poses a greater challenge. Some large or diverse group of people might read your writing—a professional committee or panel, your Facebook friends, subscribers to your blogpost—and they might have varying perspectives and levels of interest in you or in the subject of your writing. In the case of large audiences, it's often helpful to narrow your intended audience and decide which specific subset of readers you're directly addressing. Some will be an appreciative choir to whom you preach, while others will be uncertain, skeptical, or sleepy. Still others could be stark opponents or even downright hostile.

A wildly varied audience is especially difficult. Recently I had some problems with such an audience when it emerged that one of my Facebook "friends" rejected everything I posted and mocked me and my ideas. Marmaduke (let's call him) was just generally hostile toward anything posted by a teacher or educator, all of whom he viewed as loafers and parasites. He often mentioned that we had summers off, and for the half of the year during which we actually worked, we only worked a few hours a day. His message was simple: Since we're getting a "free ride" by society, we had best shut our virtual mouths. "If I make a mistake," he wrote, "thousands of dollars are lost, schedules get totally messed up, and people go ballistic. If you make a mistake, little Xinyi doesn't know how to use apostrophes or something. Who cares?" (I have eliminated Marmaduke's abusive vulgar slang.)

What to do? It made no sense to resort to name calling or vulgarities in return. I needed to shift my attention to carefully responding to Marmaduke's ideas. I tried to imagine his perspective (which, I recognize, is shared by many), I pointed out where his reasoning was flawed or his facts were incorrect, and in short methodically attempted to present a different interpretation of my profession and its value.

I'm not sure if my strategy worked. Social media can be an impersonal and precarious minefield, both dangerous and tough to navigate. You need to keep your cool. My view is that if you can get an opponent to pause even a moment before rejecting your ideas, you've essentially won. Maybe I did. Though it was only a small victory, in certain situations that's all one can hope for.

Whom Am I Writing For?
(Or, For Whom Am I Writing?)

I would like this book to be useful and interesting to a wide range of readers. I want to cast a large net here. First off, this book is for the general public, for anyone interested in improving their language, in getting their expression more exact, more polished, and more in accord with formal written English. It also might serve as a text in any number of college or high school classes on English language writing, or as a supplement for any class where writing is important and a brief, basic introduction to formal grammar and usage is necessary.

You might think that you will rarely or never have to write formal English. Perhaps not. But consider this: it's quite possible that you will find yourself having to generate reports, proposals, letters of recommendation, appeals, or articles. You might have to write an account of the car accident you were involved in. You might have to write a letter of complaint. You might feel compelled to write a letter to the editor of a newspaper or magazine. You might want to compose an article that you'll submit for publication. You will almost certainly need to write job application letters.

Alternatively, you might be writing a novel or short story—which is certainly admirable, but if that's the case, you still need to be scrupulous about your English: both publishers and literary agents strongly insist on excellent punctuation and grammar, even in fiction, where rules can be stretched, and where poetic license might permit experimentation. The takeaway? *You can stretch or break the rules but you need to know them before you do.* All of the writing situations I've mentioned—as well as countless others—require a solid command of formal written English.

My hope is that both native speakers and nonnative speakers will find this book useful. While I've aimed some sections, such as part 4 (on determiners), more at nonnative than at native speakers of English, I'm hoping that native speakers, too, might benefit from reading that section.

Stellar English can also be read purely for enjoyment: there is a story here, told through the example sentences, in which two near-future journalists, Arpita and Puneet Tagore, attempt to parse and write about the complexities of an alien invasion of the planet—an invasion by entities who neither communicate nor do any deliberate harm, yet whose presence completely disrupts life on earth.

What Is Grammar?

Grammar—the description of how a language works, how its words make up sentences and what sequences and patterns they typically follow—is not some fixed set of rules or principles. In fact, a significant portion of what professionals see as being acceptable today would certainly not have been acceptable to grammarians of the past. English grammar grows and develops year by year, even month by month. Even as I write, the language around us mutates and evolves in new ways.

As you might expect, there are multiple grammars for languages and their dialects. English speech has a grammar, Spanglish has a grammar, African American Vernacular English (AAVE) has a grammar, text-messaging has a grammar.[2] Each version of English employs a variety of complex conventions that allow users to put together clear and comprehensible messages for a specific audience.

The subdialect of English I present here, formal written English, sometimes called "standard written English" (or SWE), is the version of English that most teachers and professors expect their students to have mastered. It's the version typically used in mainstream published nonfiction, the language of legal documents, and what you're tested on in standardized tests at school. It cuts across nations and social classes, across age groups and proficiency levels, across occupations and professions. Unsurprisingly, this is the grammar that thousands of grammar handbooks seek to convey, and the one that many people long to fully grasp—and often feel bad about never having mastered.

In general, grammar books tend to "prescribe" and "proscribe." They *prescribe* a correct grammar, just as they finger-waggingly *proscribe* certain usages: Don't end a sentence with

---

[2]   In fact, the *Oxford Dictionary of African American English* is available or will be available soon. This work codifies the formal features of AAVE.

a preposition.[3] Don't split infinitives.[4] Don't start a sentence with a coordinating conjunction.[5] And here is a particularly astonishing one that I recently heard: Never use more than a single *and* in a sentence. Some people think that memorizing these prohibitions is the key to good writing. It's not. All of these prohibitions can safely be ignored with no harm to your writing style.

I am not a linguist, and my intended audience is not language specialists but, rather, people who want to write communicatively and clearly and present themselves credibly through their writing—people like you yourself. The motivating idea is that when you understand sentence-level fundamentals, you will have a solid foundation for creating paragraphs, and then it's just one more step (though not necessarily a short or simple one) into combining those paragraphs into a longer essay, report, post, or paper. Again, it's a long step, but it's one worth taking.

Formal Written English and Its Value

Let's return to Marmaduke's comment about poor Xinyi. What real-world consequences might result from her misunderstanding of apostrophe use? Marmaduke sees the issue as trivial. Xinyi might not do well in her English classes in high

---

3   These are words such as *for, as, about, to, from, against*, and the like. There are about 150 of them in English. I discuss these in more detail on pages 58–59 and 119–21.

4   Infinitives are sometimes called the "base form" of verbs: *to go, to fix, to smile*. In English they typically have a "to" preceding the word of action or of existence, but sometimes this is omitted. An infinitive cannot function as a verb in a sentence. I discuss their splitting (for example, "to *expertly* fix") on pages 84–85.

5   The words *and, but, so, or, for, nor, yet*. Sometimes *else* is included, though its use without *or* is archaic. The coordinating conjunctions and their use are examined more closely in chapter 2.

school or college. She might not score above the 10th or 20th percentile on standardized tests. Or she might be limited to going into a field that does not require any writing. Alternatively, if she has to produce written material, she might need to get someone else to edit her writing so that it's free from problems with (for example) poor apostrophe use. We all have workarounds.

But I would argue that Xinyi's lack of understanding—even of something as apparently minor as apostrophe use—actively handicaps her. It might cause her problems that she should not have to face. It might diminish her job and career prospects. It might lessen the impact or credibility of her writing, at least for some audiences. Her sloppiness with apostrophe use might make readers wary of accepting other aspects of her writing, reasoning, or presentation. It might even be the tip of a gigantic English-usage-issue iceberg. In short, her writing problems might not be as unimportant as Marmaduke suggests. She might in fact need a whole lot of help with many additional aspects of formal written English.

But not to worry. She only needs to recognize and address the problem and simply work on her formal written English fundamentals. Many courses and books are available. Admittedly, she will have to be motivated to improve her English, she'll have to work on it, and it won't be easy—you can't just read a book (like this one) and magically start to write perfect prose—but improving one's English is neither overwhelming nor impossible.

"Why bother?" you might ask. My position is that formal written English will usually stand you in good stead whenever you have to address an audience whose makeup might be diverse, wide-ranging, or unknown to you, as well as in formal situations where grammatical accuracy matters, where you need to get every single word and every mark of punctuation just right. It's a subdialect of English that has an admirable exactitude, that works well as a safe and practical default, and that is widely recognized, understood, and accepted.

Just the same, let me offer a disclaimer. People who use formal English are not necessarily smarter, more creative, or better than people who do not. This type of English doesn't have any moral, ethical, or intellectual superiority to the kind of language that, for example, you and I use every day, or the kind of language that we hear on the streets, in shops, gyms, restaurants, or TV commercials. Instead, it's a version of English that is often appropriate and effective—even necessary—to employ in certain situations. To be able to switch into it when you need to is a valuable skill.

There are two main reasons that having command over this variant of English is important, at times even crucial. First off, if you're not careful, sometimes you simply won't be understood. You need to use a language that successfully communicates your ideas. Often, written English will be unclear or will require the reader to struggle to figure out the message. Readers usually don't want to struggle to understand. Second, your English usage should reflect well on you as a thinker—that is, as a conveyor of information or knowledge. When your language, grammar, and punctuation are conventional and clear, free from obvious errors, you reinforce the idea that you're someone worth listening to.

By contrast, if you're not careful, your language will not just confuse your reader but also turn you into something of a laughingstock because your words invoke what I call an "absurd universe." To use an oft-cited example, "Let's eat, Grandma," differs quite a lot from "Let's eat Grandma." And the sentence, "I want to thank my parents, Jesus and the Virgin Mary," means something quite different from the sentence, "I want to thank my parents, Jesus, and the Virgin Mary," even though the only change in each is the addition of a comma.[6] Most people will ultimately understand your intended message, but there might be a slight pause in their understanding, maybe a chuckle, and in that short interval, sometimes you'll lose them—lose their attention, lose their confidence, lose their belief that you have something valuable to say.

Avoid Inadvertently Conjuring Up an Absurd Universe. In an earlier book, *One Day in the Life of the English Language*, I use the term *absurd universe* to describe what is invoked by many faulty sentences in English. This is a universe where a sentence describes something that is totally wacky and improbable, in fact so much so that the reader realizes that's not what's actually being described. Many times the absurd universe emerges when modification or punctuation is unclear. And while your actual message does ultimately get through, I'd argue, it's slightly marred or distorted by the fact that your reader or listener was momentarily sidetracked (possibly even amused or startled) by the absurd universe your words called up.

---

6   I discuss this issue of the "Oxford comma" (the comma prior to the *and*) in chapter 10.

In short, this book lays out the essentials that are necessary to be first, communicative, and second, trustworthy as an observer, analyst, or reporter of events.

How to Use This Book

This book is really three books in one. At its core, it's a grammar handbook that presents the fundamentals of English grammar. But at the same time it's a book that argues for the value of knowing the grammar of the subdialect, formal written English. The third book you'll find here is the one in which the example sentences tell a story.

Stellar English can thus be read in several different ways. First off, it can be used as a reference work. The material covered, including common sentence-level errors, parts of speech, punctuation, word choice, and the like, forms the essential core of a formal English grammar. The second book, implicit throughout, is the one in which I assert and argue for this grammar's utility. Sometimes this message will be explicit, but I'll try not to preach too much. The third book is the story told by its example sentences. I'm hoping that the narrative might allure you into reading the book in a way that most grammar books rarely get read: straight through, cover to cover.

Be forewarned, though, that this third book, comprising the example sentences and some short connective sections, does not constitute a typical novel. Its science-fiction world only gradually assembles itself as you read, with each passing sentence adding *some* information and moving along the narrative to an extent. As a reader of this sporadically presented story, you will have to fill in a lot of the details. Its sentences are used as examples, so a few will illustrate grammatical errors, some will be repetitious, and many will describe or invoke things/situations/people/ideas that in a traditional novel would require a lot of explanation. But the grammatical discussion and the narrative mix and intermingle in an attempt to provide a new kind of reading experience. If you want, you can simply read the narrative, ignoring the surrounding explanations. Taking in the book this way will give you more than just a story, too: you'll also be observing grammatical issues "in action" along the way.

Overview of the Book

This book is divided into seven short parts, each of which, I hope, will help you create writing that effectively communicates your ideas. These seven elements, ones you should strive for in your written English—make up what might be called the "Seven C's":

1. **Credibility**: Does your writing convey that you are trustworthy and believable?

2. **Communicativeness**: Are you successfully getting your intended message across?

3. **Complexity**: Does your language acknowledge/mirror the intricacy of the issue or problem you're addressing?

4. **Confidence**: Will your reader have certainty that you've mastered the idiom and language?

5. **Clarity**: Does your punctuation help you clearly and precisely express your ideas?

6. **Comprehensibility**: Are you employing the right words in unambiguous ways?

7. **Consequentiality**: Will what you write make some
   impact and have some importance?

All of these virtues of written English overlap, as you might
expect, so in some sense each part is about all seven. Credibility will come with clarity and communicativeness. Consequentiality will emerge when the previous six are all put
together. I separate out these individual qualities since in a
way they represent bright conceptual stars around which
issues of English grammar and usage revolve.

I will use some technical terminology, though I hope not
too much. The idea is that familiarizing you with these various terms will be useful insofar as knowing the names of
things helps us better understand, classify, and control them.
When I use a technical term, I will provide a boxed explanation of it, similar to the one that you encountered a few pages
back (page 10), in which I define "absurd universe." Using a
vocabulary of only about "ten hundred" words,[7] these twenty-
five boxes serve to explain various technical terms.

Overall, this book will offer suggestions about how to write
clear and expressive English sentences. I know that these suggestions might occasionally seem to be matters of style or
taste, the blustering of a diehard traditionalist, but bear with
me. I'm hoping that this book will lead you toward employing

---

[7]   I take this idea from Randall Munroe who, in *Thing Explainer: Complicated
Stuff in Simple Words*, uses only a thousand-word vocabulary to explain all
kinds of things, from how the blood circulates in the human body to how
washing machines work. Although Munroe does not cite him, C. K. Ogden is
the progenitor and best-known proponent of using a very simple vocabulary.
His "Basic English" program, which he laid out in the 1930s, consisted of 1,000
words. It was intended to help nonnative speakers learn English.

an English that's precise enough to clearly express what you mean, forceful enough to inspire others to action, and accurate enough so that it projects a positive, credible, and authoritative image of you, the person behind the words. In short, I want to enable you to create writing that might make a difference—writing that matters.

PART ONE
Credibility

I have already mentioned an important prerequisite to effective writing: credibility, the projection through your writing of a trustworthy person, of someone who can be believed. You want to be a "reliable narrator." A large portion of your authority will hinge on your ability to speak or write the language that your readers expect such a narrator to speak or write—and further, to do so naturally, fluently, and flawlessly. Some common errors, the ones I discuss in this part, have an exceptional importance: if you fall victim to them, your credibility as a generator of formal written English plummets.

Whenever you write something, you create an image of the author behind the words. This is called an *ethos*. What happens is that some missteps in your writing might create an *ethos*, a "me," a picture of yourself, that's not especially flattering: a picture of someone neither capable nor authoritative—someone whose poor language use might also characterize how they act and think. Making certain errors will thus not only distort or miscommunicate your message; it will also stigmatize you.

Fragments, run-ons, and *subject-verb nonagreement* are errors that fall into the stigmatizing category. These errors resemble black holes, regions of (verbal) space from which no light can escape. They're prevalent and alarming, yet difficult to describe: doing so requires backing up and explaining x, then y, and then z. But instead of having to explain the life and death of stars, the concept of the "event horizon," and the general theory of relativity, I will discuss language-related concepts that are still surprisingly complicated: what makes a sentence full or complete, how to include several sentences in one, and how various parts of a sentence should ideally fit together or match up with one another. It's their very complexity that makes these black hole–like sentences a good place to begin.

But let's come back down to earth. These three errors all stem from what is sometimes called a failure of "sentence sense"—namely, an inability to recognize what makes a group of words a sentence and how they work together as a single semantic unit. Sentences, quite simply, have some standard forms and follow certain conventional patterns. These patterns dictate your sentence's event horizon or limits, and the relation of its component parts to one another. To state it differently, you have to figure out what makes a sentence a sentence, and when, by contrast, the group of words that you've generated transforms into a verbal black hole, sucking the energy out of anyone trying to read it.

A deficiency of sentence sense stems, at least in part, from a lack of reading experience. As the novelist Gary Shteyngart puts it in his 2010 novel *Super Sad True Love Story*, some people, such as his character Eunice Park, don't really read books, but instead simply "scan them for info" (277). Many people now employ the Eunice Park technique. It's probably something picked up from years of peering at electronic devices, trying to quickly discern what's available and important on a given webpage. As you might have guessed, I believe it's much better to read than to scan—and in particular, it's beneficial to read books. Why books instead of, say, the Internet? Well, authors located via the Internet vary quite widely in terms of their language use. Some are excellent. But many others, not so much. Unlike Internet sources, books demand a sustained attention, which probably explains why it's easier to remember material read in books than it is to remember what's been read on screens.[1]

Reading books will also silently implant in you a strong "sentence sense." Most books supply example after example of what effective sentences look like, how they work, and how they flow together. Usually only published after a lengthy and rigorous review process, books are often written by people who can make the language spark and sing—can make it all but come to life. Sometimes their words seem to jump off the page and almost physically grab the reader, a reading experience that goes far beyond being merely memorable.

With that in mind, let's begin our narrative. This short opening will preview the kinds of things I talk about later on.

Engage warp drive!

---

[1] This disparity has been widely documented, though I suspect there is quite a bit of individual variation in terms of recalling screen-read texts. Jabr and Barshay provide some recent research on the issue.

Traveling[2] faster than the speed of light,[3] the alien spaceship[4] entered[5] earth's[6] atmosphere.[7]

The atmosphere slowed down the incoming[8] alien vessel,[9] but still it was traveling faster than any earth vessel, faster[10] than any object any human had ever seen.

Arpita and Puneet, dining outside at a nice restaurant in Pequa, New York,[11] saw the vessel swiftly streak across the sky.

---

[2] This is a present participle. It opens what's called a participial phrase and is modifying or describing the noun phrase that follows it. See boxed explanation, page 34.

[3] I realize that Einstein maintained that this is theoretically impossible since at the speed of light, mass approaches infinity, but please suspend your disbelief at this point.

[4] This is that noun phrase being modified by the participial phrase starting with "Traveling."

[5] This is a verb in past tense. It comes from the "infinitive" form of the verb, *to enter*.

[6] This word contains an apostrophe + s, indicating possession, ownership, or as in this case, something that's an aspect or part of something else. The atmosphere doesn't belong to earth; earth doesn't own it. But it's connected to earth, is an aspect of earth. Hence an apostrophe is needed.

[7] A few decades ago, at a writers' conference at Indiana University, George R. R. Martin led a workshop where he read some of my work. He gave me a very good piece of advice about writing science fiction: "Bring in the aliens right away." Here you go.

[8] This word functions adjectivally and looks very much like a participle, but there is no verb "to income" that it's based on. (It's a form of "to come in," but we don't say, "the coming-in alien vessel," though it's a plausible construction. See footnote about Coleridge, page 117.)

[9] Notice that I join together two full sentences (main clauses) with a comma + *but*. *But* is what is called a coordinating conjunction, and along with *and*, *so*, *or*, *for*, *nor*, and *yet*, forms the small group of words that can be used, along with a comma, to join main clauses, that is, full sentences. There are several other ways to join main clauses. See pages 49–53.

[10] These two groups of words starting with "faster," called *phrases*, are adverbial, which means that they modify a verb.

[11] These thirteen words constitute a participial or adjective phrase. Phrases differ from clauses in that a clause has a subject and a verb. Phrases do not.

"What was that?" Puneet asked.

"I have no idea," said Arpita.

"We have to check that out," Puneet proposed, putting his napkin on the table.

"No way. Not now,"[12] Arpita replied.

Puneet had stood up anxiously, but Arpita grabbed his arm and pulled him back down. "Sit. Sit," she said. "Relax."

She put her left hand palm down on the table and gently tapped the table several times to signal the password of her personal device. Suddenly her 3-D mesh-augmented-reality hologram popped up, projected from her nail-mons. She enMeshed.[13] She swiftly navigated the hologram with her right forefinger.

"Let's see," she said, peering into the space in front of her.

Puneet rolled his eyes. "Couldn't we hold off enMeshing for a little while? I mean, we're trying to have a meal here."

"Give me a minute," Arpita said, not moving her eyes away from the hologram projections she was working with.[14] "It looks to me like something pretty major is going on! All over the world, too. 'Major'

---

[12] Her response is two sentence fragments, which is acceptable in fiction but less so in formal written English.

[13] *EnMeshed* and *nail-mons* are neologisms—new, invented words. Science fiction has quite a lot of these, probably the most famous of which are Karel Čapek's *robot* and George Orwell's *doublethink*.

[14] This is an example of ending a sentence with a preposition. It's perfectly acceptable.

doesn't begin to capture it. There seems to be, like, some kind of invasion?"

Puneet watched the waitperson as she placed steaming, savory entrees in front of them.

Then he looked up at the sky. It seemed more or less normal now: quiet, cloudless, darkening. Just a contrail remained. "There's always a lot going on in the heavens," Puneet was saying. "There are about a hundred billion stars in our galaxy alone."

Arpita nodded, still enMeshed, only half-listening to her husband. She intermittently scanned the sky, which seemed quiet and unremarkable at the moment. She disEnmeshed. False alarm, probably.

"And[15] there are about a hundred billion galaxies at least." He paused.

"I'm not sure of that number, darling," Arpita responded.

"So[16] that means that there are one hundred billion times one hundred billion stars."

She said, "Why are you bothering with all these numbers right now? We're just trying to have a nice dinner! And maybe the world is being invaded!"

They seemed to be swapping positions, each telling the other to relax.

Puneet paused. "Oh. Sorry. But you were not actually eating." He looked around him at the other diners, all of whom seemed engaged with one another

---

[15]   This is an example of starting a sentence with a coordinating conjunction. Many people have been taught not to do this, but it's OK to do occasionally.

[16]   Another example of starting a sentence with a coordinating conjunction. This is generally more acceptable in speech than in formal writing.

or with their food. He went on. "But hey, a lot of stars. A nearly unfathomable number of stars.[17] What I'm trying to say," Puneet continued, realizing he had Arpita's attention, and speaking in a voice slightly above a whisper, "is that we have all these galaxies, and in them, a myriad of stars and planets. I don't know the name of the number, but there are so many stars and planets."

"I know that a googol[18] is one followed by a hundred zeros," Arpita noted. "A googolplex is one followed by a googol of zeros."

"Are you just trying to be annoying?" Puneet asked.

"No, I'm just trying to eat."

"Right," said Puneet. "So let's say that there are maybe ten sextillion stars," he offered. "I think that's the name of the number. Now, of that many stars, how many have a habitable planet orbiting around them? Let's say it's one in a million. That means that there are one followed by sixteen zeros habitable planets are out there."

Arpita went back to her plank salmon, but Puneet pushed aside his gnocchi, which was too salty to consume, and continued, "In the mid-twentieth century, an American astrophysicist named Frank Drake came up with a formula called the 'Drake equation,' which offers us a blueprint for figuring out how many habitable planets there are in the universe."

---

[17]   Both of these are fragments also, but acceptable and understandable in fiction. It's best to limit their use in nonfiction.

[18]   This is not to be confused with "google" (the search engine), nor is "googolplex" to be confused with "googleplex" (HQ of Google).

Puneet enMeshed, angling the projection from his hands so that Arpita could see it.

Hovering in the air was the following equation:

$$N = (R^*) \times (fp) \times (ne) \times (fl) \times (fi) \times (fc) \times (L)$$

Arpita pointedly ignored what her husband was projecting.[19]

"They said there would be no math," she said.

"Yes, but who exactly are 'they'?" Puneet asked.[20]

He disEnmeshed, took a bite of his gnocchi. "But I want to share this idea with you—and also share the second most famous equation of all time." Arpita didn't ask, but he added, "after $E = mc^2$." He paused. "There are so many habitable planets that it is mathematically, virtually,[21] and literally[22] impossible that we are alone in the universe."

---

[19] Here is what he projected:

    N: The number of civilizations in the Milky Way galaxy whose electromagnetic emissions are detectable.

    R*: The rate of formation of stars suitable for the development of intelligent life (number per year).

    fp: The fraction of those stars with planetary systems.

    ne: The number of planets, per solar system, with an environment suitable for life.

    fl: The fraction of suitable planets on which life actually appears.

    fi: The fraction of life-bearing planets on which intelligent life emerges.

    fc: The fraction of civilizations that develop a technology that produces detectable signs of their existence.

    L: The average length of time such civilizations produce such signs (years). (Shostak)

[20] Puneet is noting an example of a problem with pronoun reference. Arpita's joke is that there is no antecedent for "they."

[21] Comma prior to the *and* (or the *or*) in a list is called the Oxford or serial comma. Some disciplines require its use; others prohibit it. Much controversy surrounds its use.

[22] "Literally" has entered our current discourse to an alarming extent. I'm not sure why. Perhaps in this virtual age people are trying to emphasize and em-

Above them, more super-fast streaks of light, lots of them, crisscrossed in the sky.

Quite abruptly, life on the planet earth all changed.

Everyone knew it, too.

---

brace the literal or actual? Bryan A. Garner remarks, "When *literally* is used figuratively—to mean 'emphatically,' 'metaphorically,' or the like—the word is stretched paper-thin (but not literally)" (568).

1

Sentence-Level Issues

FRAGMENTS

Sometimes, short and apparently simple sentences fail because they are "incomplete": they are *sentence fragments*. While acceptable in fiction, print advertisements, text messages, or casual e-mails, sentence fragments rarely bolster the effectiveness of formal writing. Quite the opposite.[1] Too easily misunderstood, they damage your credibility. Fragments can make your writing seem like shorthand or a text message rather than a serious statement.

I should point out too that a long sentence can be a fragment. Sentence length has no direct connection to completeness or incompleteness. You can have a fifty-word fragment or a one-word sentence.

Here, I have cast the ongoing story entirely in fragments. I have tried to make it as communicative as possible. This experiment will give you an idea of both how the fragment does not really work and also of how, when stretched to limits of acceptability, language can deliver unusual effects:

[1]   Note that this is itself a fragment. Would the sentence, "Actually, quite the opposite is the case" be better? You decide. This book is not totally "formal" in its language use, so perhaps the fragment is preferable. Sorry if all this seems overly meta.

Left the restaurant. Definite endpoint reached. No more good feelings from the wine, from the pleasant atmosphere, or from the expensive, intricately spiced, prepared food. No, none of that: the indulgence of relaxation all forgotten, dissipated. Although they knew that something had changed. Something major and overwhelmingly important. Still alone in a foreign land, really. No, not India, not home. Nothing like it in fact. Yes, they and their world . . . never the same. Ended?

And then—? What?

Puneet, wanting to enMesh. Too connected to it, too reliant on it. Felt like an addict. In a world full of addicts.

Puneet: "The Drake equation. A hundred billion inhabited planets in the Milky Way. Many life forms similar to ours. . . ." A speech slowing, a gradual trailing off. Restarting: "Sorry. But it looks—"

"It?"

"I mean, these spaceships, these things in the sky—"

Arpita: "Right. Whatever. But alien visitors—? On earth? Here now? Among us?" EnMeshed now. Again.

While Puneet looked at her. Even as they stopped, right in the middle of the sidewalk. Which, despite the crowdedness. Intense, high-affect dyadic encounter taking place between married couple. "Yes. Aliens. Maybe. Unless something else is going on, perhaps." Her left hand projecting Mesh, his words hovering in the air, like different kinds of space vessels, sort of. "Only in the US?"

Arpita's response wearily delivered. "Unlikely." To state the extremely obvious. DisEnmeshed. Even though she hoped that back home it might be different.

Safe. "My plan for tomorrow's column: an opinion piece about the 'American Dream.' Hah! Out the window!"

"Not so fast." Puneet's voiced opinion. Gathering, gathering his thoughts. "Look, since you believe in your idea about the American Dream, since you want to write it." Not sure how to end, so after a brief pause, "On the other hand, relevance of anything right now is—?"

While composed in fragments, this narrative is nonetheless almost completely understandable. But is it good? I find it off-putting and annoying to read. In addition to a "meaning," it conveys either a lack of familiarity with how the language works, or an attempt to convey, via obvious distortions of grammar, something of the weirdness of what the characters are experiencing. Evelyn Nien-Ming Ch'ien notes in her provocative and influential book *Weird English* that sometimes "the violence to grammatical conventions reflects the state of mind of the protagonist" (58). In fiction, which often experiments with language, such deformations can sometimes work, at least for some readers, but in formal written English, weird English is often just, well, too weird.

It's best to write using full sentences. I'll continue the narrative here in full-sentence mode, retaining the fragment-style only at the end:

Walking to their car, Arpita stopped and grabbed her husband, both of her hands on his arms. "What are you saying, then? What do we do?"

"We keep on working. We keep on writing. This is all probably nothing, I mean nothing out of the ordinary. We need to figure out what it is, though, and we need to write about it and inform others. That's our job, you know, what we're paid for."

Arpita, her beautiful dark eyes locking onto those of her husband, looked up at him, her five-foot-six dwarfed by his six-foot-four. She could see her face reflected in his dilated pupils. "You're right," she said. "Writing is what we do. In all other ways we're powerless. I really wish we were back home, though."

"I do too. But we're not. And our biggest problem is this." He pointed to the sky. They both looked up to see a newly formed gridwork of vivid, multicolored contrails indicative of incoming vessels clearly not of earthly origin. "That's what we have to worry about."

"That's what we're going to figure out," Arpita replied. "That's the American Dream, isn't it? Figuring out what the world is really like and then—what? Trying to make it right. Maybe I can still write that column. It'll be a lot different from what I'd planned!" Since there was no table, she lifted her left hand, palm up, and curled her fingers in, touching them in her password. She enMeshed. The monitors beneath each fingernail projected the 3-D augmented reality. She subvocalized a search. "Says here that thousands of UAPs have entered our atmosphere, moving at unearthly speeds, and landing all over the planet."

Puneet stared. "What?"

"An alien invasion," Arpita said. Then she paused. "We've got a lot to write about all of a sudden."

"Yes, that's right," Puneet agreed, hugging her tightly to him. "That seems to be what we do here."

"Yes," Arpita said. "Oh yes." She then prayed to Hanuman. Puneet joined her.

What Constitutes a Full Sentence?

I recommend that in any formal writing that you need to do, write using full sentences. There are three elements to a full sentence:

1. A noun, pronoun, or noun phrase, which will function as the subject;

2. A verb;

3. A tense for that verb.

This sounds simple but in fact requires quite a lot of explanation. I don't want to be in the category of the guy you ask what time it is and who tells you how to build a clock, but in this situation it probably is a good idea to look at component parts.

I will use a "thumbs-up" emoji (👍) before an example sentence that is acceptable as formal written English; a "thumbs-down" emoji (👎) signifies the opposite. Sometimes I will combine these two emojis to suggest something between acceptable and not acceptable, maybe an area where language-use rules are debatable: (👎👍 or 👍👍👎 or 👎👎👍).

Here are four complete sentences, the component parts of which I will discuss in the text boxes that follow:

👍 Arpita and Puneet drove a beautiful, four-motor electric Andromeda Ionosph.

👍 The car was parked in the somewhat grimy, ill-lighted municipal lot.

👍 Arpita ran up to it and saw that it was ticketed.

👍 She somehow knew this would happen.

A **noun** is a person, place, or thing. A "thing" need not be an object you can touch. It can be something like *thought, passion, idea, instinct*. Most nouns are called **common nouns.** *Car* and *lot* are common nouns. A name is a **proper noun.** *Arpita, Puneet*, and *Andromeda Ionosph* are all proper nouns.

A **noun phrase** is the noun together with a few words following it or preceding it. *Beautiful, four-motor electric Andromeda Ionosoph* is a noun phrase, as is *somewhat grimy, ill-lighted municipal lot*.

A **pronoun** substitutes for a noun or noun phrase. According to a well-known linguist, the late Gerald Nelson, "pronouns are a subclass of nouns" (36), which is a good way to look at them. Pronouns that can function as subjects include *I, you, he, she, it, we, they* (subject pronouns); and also words like *that, those, these, this*; or *anyone, everyone, someone, no one*. Note that not all pronouns can be subjects.[2]

The **subject** of a sentence usually, though not always, is placed early in the sentence since it is the focus, the hero, the protagonist, or principal actor of the sentence, and its upfront placement immediately alerts the reader to that very fact. The subject is the **noun** (person, place, or thing), **noun phrase, or pronoun** that is doing something or whose state of being is described. In the three example sentences, the subjects are *Arpita and Puneet* (proper noun), *car* (common noun), *It* (pronoun), and *She* (pronoun).

Sometimes the subject is implied, as in command forms. Puneet might yell at this stage, "Take that ticket off our windshield!" with the subject being an implicit "You."

The verb form is also a crucial element. Admittedly, we often encounter language that does not include verb forms: "One Way," "Exit," "Ten Items or Less." But formal, written English requires a verb in each sentence. In addition, make sure that your verb indicates a specific time period during which the action of the sentence takes place—past, present, or future. That is, make sure your verb has a *tense*. But maybe you're wondering just what a verb or tense is. The following boxed section supplies some details.

A **verb** is a word either denoting action or indicating a state of being. In the preceding example sentences, the verbs are *drove, was parked, ran, was ticketed,* and *knew.* The action a verb shows can be physical, like *drove*; or mental, like *knew.* In addition, verbs can show states of being, such as *feel, sense, become, exist,* or *is/are/was/were.* This last group, *to be* verbs, can also describe a state of action, like *was parked,* or *was ticketed.*

Tense is the form of the verb indicating when (at what time period) the events of the sentence are happening or existing: present, past, or future. In English, there are these three main tenses and variations of each.[3] All the example sentences are in past tense.

Sometimes the subject is the doer or experiencer of the action. The verbs used in this situation are in **active voice**: *Puneet and Arpita drove a beautiful four-engine Air Andromeda. She somehow knew this would happen.*

At other times, the subject receives the action. Verbs used when this is the case are said to be in the **passive voice**: *The car was parked. It was ticketed.*[4]

---

[3] See table 1, page 64.
[4] I discuss the passive voice in more detail on pages 80–84.

Here are some more examples of full sentences. You will see that each has a *noun* that functions as the sentence's *subject*, as well as a *verb* and a *tense*:

👍 Arpita looked at the sky. [*Arpita* is the subject, the doer; *looked* is the verb; past tense.]

👍 Puneet tapped through his nail-mons, noting how his heart rate, breathing, and blood pressure had all risen. [Here, *Puneet* is the subject, the doer; *tapped* is the verb; past tense. There is a second sentence embedded within the first, too, and it also has a subject, verb, and tense: *his heart rate, breathing, and blood pressure* make up the subject, and *had risen* is the verb. This too takes place in the past, the tense being a form of past tense called past perfect.[5]]

👍 Their nail-mons provided information about a hundred or more body functions. [*Nail-mons* is the subject; *provided* is the verb; past tense.]

👍 They also had the ability to act as projectors of the Mesh, or as phones, compasses, flashlights, alarms, and many other things. [*They* is the subject and *had* is the verb here. Tense is past.]

The four following example sentences take a slightly different form. They include a *to be* verb expressing an ongoing state of being. The verbs are all in present tense, and each has an initial noun or noun phrase functioning as each sentence's subject:

---

[5]   Discussed in more detail in the chapter on verbs, pages 64 and 67–69.

👍 The earth **is** imperiled.

👍 Our times **are** vexed.

👍 They **are struggling** against an unknown invader.

👍 Qarqangaarjuk Akbaliatuk **is** president, the first Inuit to hold that office.

Imperiled and *vexed* are what are called past participles in the example sentences; *struggling* is what's called a present participle. The first two sentences each include an adjective that describes the subject. *Are struggling* is a verb phrase of action that says what the subject, *they*, is doing. In the fourth sentence, the verb *is* indicates a present state of being. For some definitions of the words *participle* and *adjective*, check ahead to the next text box.

To return once again to a crucial point, make sure that your sentence's verb indicates pastness, presentness, or futurity. Again, a full sentence must have a *tense*.

👍 The couple suddenly **realized** the importance of **surrounding** events. [Past tense using participle (*realized*). The participle *surrounding* is used as an adjective here, modifying the noun, *events*.] 👍 The aliens **were evidently landing** in many vessels. [Past tense using participle, *landing*.]

👍 It **will be** a brave new world. [Future tense.]

👎 The aliens landing in many vessels. [The participial form by itself here does not convey a tense. One way to revise this might be *The aliens landed in many vessels*. Or you can just insert a *to be* verb prior to *landing*: *The aliens* were *landing in many vessels*.]

Participles are words formed from verbs. The present participle usually ends in *-ing* (*running, rowing, writing*). The past participle usually ends in *-ed* or *-en*. (But some past participles are irregular, such as *become, brought, caught, drunk, felt, flown, got* or *gotten, known, gone, led, laid, lain, ridden, rung, seen, sung, slept, swum, thrown, won, written.*)

A participle can do one of three things:

1. On the most basic level, it can simply show action or a state of being; that is, it can function as a verb:

   👍 "Arpita and Puneet both **seemed** very worried.

2. It can also function as an **adjective,** a word that describes, gives details about, or restricts the meaning of a noun, and thus can highlight, animate, or describe certain aspects of a noun.[6]

   👍 "It was a **frightening** situation." [*Frightening* modifies *situation*.]

   👍 "**Looking** at her messages and **alarmed** by the events taking place, Arpita broke down." [The bold words describe what she is doing (*looking*) and feeling (*alarmed*).]

3. In addition, a participle can come after a verb showing a state of being (usually *is, was, were, been, has, had,* or *have*) and combine with it in order to convey a slightly complex time frame. These three following sentences, for example, all indicate something that started in the past and that continues into the present:

   👍 Puneet said, "I **have decided** that we need to investigate in person."

   👍 Arpita **was crying**. "In person? Let's research the Mesh first."

   👍 "Have you **been listening** to me at all, darling? The Mesh is behind the curve. It's yesterday's news."

---

[6]   I devote chapter 5 to adjectives, pages 113–24.

Typical Sentence Constructions That Result in Fragments

While there are many variations of incomplete sentences, I want to look at the most typical ways that sentences fail to be complete:

1. When instead of using a tensed verb, the writer uses a participle (a word like *running* or *going*, which is derived from a verb, to be sure, but which, as I note in the preceding box, cannot by itself function as a verb);

2. When the writer inserts a word like *while*, *because*, *since*, or *unless* before a complete sentence;

3. When the writer uses *which* as a subject;

4. When the writer uses *although* as a substitute for *however* to open a sentence; and

5. When the writer uses a Q/A format, and the answer lacks subject, verb, or both.

I'll look at these one by one.

To Be Avoided: Fragments Caused by Misuse of Participles

Adjectives have no tense. Thus, participles, when used as adjectives, need a verb like *was* or *were* attached to them so that they can function as a verb in a sentence. Participles are formed from verbs but are not verbs in and of themselves. None of the following work:

👎 People **longing** to go back to the past.

👎 **Running** up to landing sites.

👎 **Infuriated** by all the sudden changes.

👎 **Having** no idea what happened.

👎 **Desired** by most people.

While you must make sure that your sentence includes a tensed verb form, you also should make sure that your sentence includes a subject—namely, a person or entity that does, did, or will do (or be) something. You can transform the preceding fragments into complete sentences by simply adding verbs and/or subjects. I have boldfaced the additions needed to transform these thumbs-down fragments into complete sentences:

👍 People **are always** longing to go back to the past, Puneet thought. [Present.]

👍 **He saw people** running up to landing sites. [Past.]

👍 Infuriated by all the sudden changes, **angry citizens called the local police**. [Past.]

👍 Having no idea what happened, **many people were glued to their televisions and continuously en-Meshed since the invasion took place**. [Past.]

👍 **Although they were** desired by most people, **explanations for the invasion were not forthcoming**. [Past.]

The five short thumbs-down fragments I'm dealing with here could well be part of longer, more complex sentences, too:

👍 Puneet usually resented people longing to go back to a world that no longer exists, but now he felt a shared common cause with them. [Now the subject is "Puneet," and the verb "resented." The tense is past. Note that this example shows how two complete sentences can be joined as one. The part of the sentence following "but" can stand on its own as a sentence: "Now he felt a shared common cause with them." The subject is "he" and the verb "felt" (past tense).]

👍 Driving home, they saw many people, oblivious of the potential danger, running up to landing sites. ["They" is the subject. The verb here is "saw," and the tense is past.]

👍 Overwhelmed by what looked like terrifying changes in his world, one man screamed. ["One man" is the subject; "screamed" is the verb. This is past tense also. Note the long participial phrase that starts this sentence ("Overwhelmed by . . .). Within that phrase is the present participle, *terrifying*, modifying *changes*.]

To Be Avoided: Fragments Created by Starting a Sentence with a Word Like *If*, *Since*, *Unless*, or *While*

The first word of a sentence is very important. Words like "How," "What," "When," "Why," or "Where" typically mark the start of a question. "I" generally will start a sentence that offers an opinion or personal experience. "But" will often start a sentence in which a writer or speaker wants to make a contrast, offer an objection, or introduce some additional element or issue.

Other opening words, subordinators, signal something that might seem a little counterintuitive. They signal that that the first part of a sentence is sort of secondary importance. It's information that the writer or speaker mentions but which they will shortly set aside in favor of something that is more important and that will come later in the sentence. The opener is "subordinate to" the upcoming main idea. This is called a *subordinate* or *dependent clause*.

Here are a few common subordinators: *after, although, as, as if, as long as, soon as, because, before, despite the fact that, if, in order that, provided that, since, so that, though, till, unless, until, when, where, while.* If you use one of these at the start of a sentence, the words that directly follow it, even though they have a subject, a verb, and a tense, will **not** make a full sentence. Subordinator + sentence = fragment (👎). That resultant fragment leaves the reader hanging, waiting for something to complete it. How to get a 👍 ? Simply add a comma and a complete sentence:

👍 Although people worried, they survived.
(Subordinator + subject + tensed verb + comma + subject + tensed verb).

Subordinators can appear in many different spots in a sentence. Note that in my fragments-only narrative (pp. 26–27), many of the sentence fragments start with a subordinator. That's what makes them fragments.

A **clause** is a group of words containing a subject and a verb. It does not have to be a full sentence. There are many types of clauses in English. They can function as nouns, adjectives, or other parts of speech. A clause that can stand on its own as a full sentence is called a **main clause** or an **independent clause**. If you have a main clause, though, and place a present participle or subordinator in front of it, this transforms the main clause into a **subordinate** or **dependent clause**.

Not too surprisingly, the words introducing that first not-so-important part are called **subordinators** or **subordinating conjunctions**; they subordinate, diminish, reduce the importance of the first part of the sentence, at the same time as they set up and prepare the reader for the main idea.

Here are two examples of how to correctly use subordinators:

👍 Thinking their calm and comfortable life was over, Arpita and Puneet fell into a strange funk that first day of the invasion. [This sentence starts with a present participle, *thinking*, which begins a participial clause (that is, dependent or subordinate clause) of eight words. It modifies *Arpita and Puneet*. What follows is a main clause.]

👍 While they were absorbed in their own troubled thoughts, they simultaneously realized that as journalists their responsibility was to find out what was going on. [This sentence starts with *while*, which is a subordinator, thus making the words up to the comma a dependent or subordinate clause. The main clause starts with *they simultaneously realized . . .*]

The following are some sample sentence fragments (ones opening with a subordinator), which need a full sentence added to them in order to be full sentences:

👎 Because Puneet and Arpita just had a nice meal. [Maybe replace the period with a comma, and add something like, *they were less inclined to be worried than most people*. Or just omit *because*.]

☞ Although there were warning signs all over. [A possible way to complete this sentence could be, after turning the period into a comma, *most people still went about their daily business.*]

☞ While they were driving home. [Delete period. Perhaps add comma plus *something truly amazing happened in the skies overhead.*]

Subordinators offer variety and also can provide some complexity, showing (among other things) cause and effect, a concession, a significant contrast, or simultaneity. They might provide some background information that has some relevance or importance. But, again, using them requires you to attach a brand-new full sentence to the sentence fragment your subordinator has created.

👍 *When* the challenges piled up, Puneet and Arpita went into a take-no-prisoners mode. [Cause-effect.]

👍 *Even though* their car cost them a year's salary, it was worth it. [Concession.]

👍 *While* the skies above were menacing, they felt quite comfortable floating along in their luxurious Andromeda. [Contrast.]

👍 *As* Puneet drove, the sky filled up. [Simultaneity.]

Just to give you a sense of how all these sentences work, I will break down the last sentence into its component parts:

As [subordinator] + Puneet [proper noun functioning as subject] + drove [past tense of *to drive*], the sky [noun functioning as subject]+ filled up [past tense of *to fill up*].

More schematically . . .

Subordinator + proper noun + tensed verb + comma + noun + tensed verb

To Be Avoided: Starting a Sentence with *Which*

Beginning a sentence with *which* will usually result in a fragment because *which* cannot by itself be the subject of a sentence. (*Which* may start a question or a noun phrase, however.) Starting with *which* usually creates a dependent clause, one that will typically occur later in a sentence.

- 👎 Which is what we want.
- 👎 Which was beginning to ramp up and could be dangerous.
- 👍 Which do we want?
- 👍 Which country was most severely affected was a matter of debate. [The sentence is essentially a question embedded within a declarative sentence: "Which country was most severely affected?"]

The usual situation with *which* is as follows: the **subordinate** or **dependent clause** that *which* starts typically follows a main clause to which it's attached with a comma:

- 👍 At least they were together, **which** was a relief.
- 👍 Arpita was especially worried about public anxiety, **which** was likely to ramp up and could be dangerous.

Here is another classification of types of clauses. An **essential clause**, also referred to as a **restrictive clause**, is one that's *absolutely necessary* for the sentence to convey its meaning. A **nonrestrictive** or **nonessential clause** is one that provides some additional information but which is *not needed to convey the main idea* of the sentence. Here are two sentences that highlight the difference between essential and nonessential clauses. I've italicized the clauses.

ESSENTIAL or RESTRICTIVE:

Their next-door neighbor, Garrastazu, hated reporters *who were nosy and opinionated.*

[THIS MEANS that he hated *only* nosy, opinionated reporters. The second part of the sentence is *essential* for conveying the meaning; it specifies the particular sort of reporters he hates.]

NONESSENTIAL or NONRESTRICTIVE:

Their next-door neighbor, Garrastazu, hated reporters, *who were nosy and opinionated.*

[THIS MEANS that he hated *all reporters*; the second part of the sentence is *not essential* to conveying this main message, though it does give some possible reason for Garrastazu's feelings. It just adds some extra information, specifically that reporters are nosy and opinionated.]

The two clauses in the preceding examples (the group of words beginning with "who") are called *relative clauses*; they function as adjectives and refer to or modify the noun *reporters.*

That, in contrast to *which*, can function as a subject:

👍 A lot of spaceships had already landed. That was worrisome.

👎 Which was very worrisome indeed. [Fragment.]

While *that* usually starts a main or an essential clause and *which* typically starts a dependent or nonessential one, *which* is being used more and more to begin an essential clause, a development that many readers disapprove of.

👍 Looking at the night sky had been something that he liked. [Essential clause: *that he liked.*]

👍 👎 Looking at the night sky had been something which he liked. [Essential clause: *which he liked. That* is still preferable in formal English.]

While *which* can be used to introduce an essential clause, many word processing programs, not to mention teachers and editors, will flag it. In general, it's best to use *that* for essential elements and *which* for nonessential ones.[7]

To Be Avoided: Using *Although* instead of *However*

As I suggest earlier, *although* works in the same way as *while* and the many other subordinators that I list on page 38. When a sentence begins with *although*, it must have a second

---

[7]   Both Benjamin Dreyer and Bryan A. Garner agree with me about this, the latter suggesting that nine times out of ten, you should use either a comma + *which* with nonessential elements and a *that* with essential ones (900). However, both of these respected writers (the first an editor and the second a law professor and grammarian) admit that not all writers abide by the rule, which Dreyer notes some see as "pushily constrictive" (34) and Garner admits is often not followed in British English.

clause in it, this second part being a full sentence. Both of the following show how *although* correctly functions:

👍 Although he was nearly middle-aged, Puneet was still youthful. [First part of sentence, if it ended in a period after *middle-aged*, would be a fragment. After the comma, there is a full sentence.]

👍 Although she was the same age as her colleagues, Arpita looked much younger, perhaps because she regularly practiced yoga. [Again, the first part of the sentence, if it ended on a period after *colleagues*, would be a fragment. The second part, after the first comma, is a full sentence.]

I separate out *although* since I have noticed that many people now (incorrectly) use this particular subordinator as a synonym for *however*:

👍 However, it's obviously a world in which the Mesh will help people cope. [Some experts object to starting a sentence with *however*, but there is nothing grammatically or stylistically wrong with it. Using it implies a contrast that you are drawing (in this example sentence, with some previously mentioned idea that the Mesh is, perhaps, annoying, or too pervasive).]

👍 Although it's obviously a world in which the Mesh helps people cope, most people are struggling to go about their daily business as if nothing had happened. [Subject: *most people*. Verb: *are struggling*. Tense: a version of present called present progressive.]

👎 Although, it's obviously a world in which the Mesh helps people cope. [The comma does not undo the

subordinator function of *although*. You need to attach
a full sentence to this. You also should delete the
comma after *although*.]

This misusage of *although* (with the comma following it in
the preceding 𝒫 example sentence) replicates some people's
spoken English, where the word's second syllable is heavily
accented and drawn out: al-THOUGH (pause). In written
English, however, we can't quite replicate that emphasis, and
although always functions as a subordinator.

To Be Avoided: Incomplete Sentences as Answers to Questions

Sometimes you will be in the situation where you pose a question and then offer an answer. You need to make sure that
the answer is a full sentence.

> 𝒫 What really changed people's lives, though? The Mesh
> and the nail-mons. [Should be something like *What
> really changed people's lives, though, were the Mesh and
> the nail-mons.*]

> 𝒫 Even though the Mesh made people's lives easier,
> what did it simultaneously do damage to? Relation-
> ships. [Should be *Even though the Mesh made
> people's lives easier, it simultaneously did damage to
> relationships.*]

Fragments for Effect

It's only fair to note that sometimes fragments can be used to
create a dramatic effect, particularly in works of fiction. Kolln,
Gray, and Salvatore discuss what they call "deliberate sentence

fragments," and note, "Experienced writers know how to use them effectively—noun phrases or verb phrases that invariably call attention to themselves" (318). Their use of the phrase "experienced writers" tips their collective hand: citing examples from fiction by Sandra Cisneros and John le Carré, the authors offer a subtle "don't try this at home" element to their advice.

But I will try. Many readers would likely accept the following deliberate fragment:

> 👍 👎 The situation was reminiscent of how the world changed after the dropping of the first atomic bombs. Anguished, burning, filled with regret. [Setting off the fragment in this way might be more rhetorically effective than using a colon to connect it to the sentence.]

Some readers might accept the two-word sentence fragment ending this thought:

> 👍 👎 👎 The alien vessels came down, landing in many countries. Including ours.

I give this sentence an emoji that indicates acceptance by (my guess) one-third of an audience for formal written English. The argument for the usage would be that ending on a fragment emphasizes a strong or bold statement, making it more visible than it would be if it were simply appended to the lead sentence after a comma.

In many language situations—informal ones such as in many e-mails and text messages, as well as in novels, short stories, or plays, fragments abound and are acceptable:

👍 "Hey!"

👍 "Never."

👍 "Huh?"

But, again, this kind of usage rarely appears in formal written English.

2

Sentence-Level Issues

RUN-ONS AND SUBJECT-VERB AGREEMENT

As my discussion of subordinators probably implied, writers will often combine two or more sentences into one longer sentence. Such a practice is reasonable and often desirable since it lets you create a variety of sentence lengths and patterns. A mix of short, medium, and long sentences—as well as a mix of sentence structures—tends to make writing more interesting to read.

There are a variety of ways to effectively combine multiple sentences into a single one that brings together two or more distinct but related ideas. But let me offer a caveat. As you join sentences, you must clearly indicate where the break between the sentences you're connecting occurs, and, since you're linking two or more sentences, you also need to help the reader understand the relationship between them. To rephrase, you've got to signal your reader where some new idea is starting—and also make sure that the linkage you're making helps you get your meaning across.

For example, these two sentences might be ones you want to connect:

👍 Many alien spaceships had landed.

👍 They did not appear to be aggressive.

Here are some acceptable ways to join these two short sentences, ways that both allow your reader to understand your idea and that effectively sustain your credibility:

1. Use a semicolon. This suggests a close connection between the two sentences or main clauses. It's a way, perhaps, of anticipating an emotional response to the first sentence and swiftly trying to alleviate the scariness by tightly linking a second sentence:

    👍 The alien spaceships had landed; they did not appear to be aggressive.

2. Use a coordinating conjunction and a comma.

The following words are **coordinating conjunctions**: *and, but, so, or, for, nor, yet*. You can remember these by using ABSOFNY, though some might prefer FANBOYS or something else.

These small words are very important and can indicate addition (*and*), opposition (*or*), concession (*but, yet*), consequence (*so, for*), or negation (*nor*).

In terms of joining the example sentences, *and, but,* and *yet* would all work. Each has a slightly different meaning, with *but* and *yet* being the most obvious choices since they ease the fear that the first sentence creates:

👍 The alien spaceships had landed, but they did not appear to be aggressive.

3. Make one clause subordinate to the other (that is, use a subordinator). This repeats the strategy of use 2, introducing a scary actuality and following it with a swiftly delivered relief:

   👍 Although alien spaceships had landed, they did not appear to be aggressive.

   👍 The alien spaceships had landed, though they did not appear to be aggressive.

4. Rephrase, using an internal *which* clause (making that clause nonessential). This seems to offer a more neutral record of events, with less attempt at lessening readers' fears:

   👍 The alien spaceships, which did not immediately appear to be aggressive, had landed.

5. Use *however* + a semicolon. (This is a version of use 1, earlier, but still worthy of mention; it emphasizes a contrast that the writer is making.)

   👍 The alien spaceships had landed; however, they did not appear to be aggressive.

   However is not an "ABSOFNY" word. It often (though not always) functions in a somewhat similar way. If you opt for a *however* instead of *but* or *yet* in these kinds of sentence constructions, keep in mind that unlike the coordinating conjunctions, *however* requires a semicolon before it.[1] A comma won't do.

---

[1] These guidelines also apply to other conjunctive adverbs that might be used, such as *consequently*, *nevertheless*, or *on the other hand*. See pages 130–33 for a discussion of such words.

6. Make into a single main clause. (This will sometimes not be possible, but here it's no problem.)

👍 Many alien spaceships, all apparently nonaggressive, had landed.

When you have two full sentences that you include in one sentence, you need to make sure that you punctuate your sentence with care. If you join those two sentences with just a comma, or if you omit punctuation entirely, you are likely to have created a *run-on sentence*. This is *not* generally acceptable in formal English. In the following, the first example is of a *comma splice*; the second, a *fused sentence*.

1. Avoid joining the two sentences with just a comma:

👎 The alien spaceships had landed, they did not appear to be aggressive. [*Comma splice.*]

2. Avoid joining the two sentences with no punctuation between them:

👎 The alien spaceships had landed they did not appear to be aggressive. [*Fused sentence.*]

Run-on sentences are a common problem. They make your writing resemble a "stream of consciousness." While long acceptable in fiction, such a technique rarely works in nonfictional prose. Run-on sentences force readers to pause, go back, and reread. Readers generally don't like doing that. Further, if a meaning eventually emerges, it might not be your intended meaning. Disrupting the usual sequential reading process is not likely to endear you to an audience, boost your credibility, or help convey your message.

Acceptable Sentence Connections
Using Just Commas

It's acceptable to connect two sentences using only commas if the sentences are very short. Here, for example, is the title of a 2005 book by Jan Harold Brunvand:

👍 *Be Afraid, Be Very Afraid.*

Brunvand's title comes from a line in the 1986 movie *The Fly*, a line usually represented as two separate sentences. (The example is a little unfair since it's a title, but the title will "work" as a sentence, so I am offering it as a possibility.)

Another acceptable way for the comma to join sentences is when the sentences form a list or series of more than two sentences. This works only if each main clause is simple (that is, has no internal punctuation).

👍 Some people gawped and shouted, others fell to their knees, and still others recorded the unprecedented events on a nail-mons app.

Note that omitting all punctuation (creating a doubly fused sentence) won't work. Commas will effectively separate the three sentences of your list, but there are no acceptable fused sentences.

Some writers and editors accept commas (rather than semicolons) as a way to join two main clauses when the second sentence reverses the meaning of the first:

👆👍 The people of earth were not merely alarmed, they were terrified.

👆👎 The events were more than merely memorable, they were life changing.

I give these constructions a "thumbs-up/thumbs-down" emoji because a number of readers won't accept them. Some will. Keep in mind that a safer choice than the comma would be a semicolon—or a conversion of the one sentence into two.[2]

Similarly, a "tag question," that is, a sentence with a short question appended at the end, contains two main clauses connected with only a comma, and this is an acceptable construction (though it's usually found only in informal English):

👍 "It's been a scary time, hasn't it?" Arpita asked her husband.

👍 "You want to leave, don't you?" Puneet responded, thinking wistfully of their village in India.

In general . . .

Using run-on sentences, except in the situations I've noted, damages your credibility as a writer and thinker. While some readers won't notice, others might think of you as someone who writes in a slapdash manner, or who thinks in a stream-of-consciousness way, with your thoughts all flowing together in an oft-incomprehensible mish-mash. Neither response will help you get your point across.

---

[2] For example, the oft-consulted Grammarly website offers the following as an example of an unacceptable comma splice: "Koala bears are not actually bears, they are marsupials." While I agree that this is not acceptable, the second clause does reverse the meaning of the first (in a way completing its message), and thus the sentence will be seen as acceptable by many writers and editors. You need to be careful with this, though.

Make Sure That Your Subjects and Verbs "Agree" with Each Other

When a subject *agrees with* a verb, this means that the words being used grammatically match up with one another; they fit together in a way that reinforces the information your sentence provides. You should say, 👍 "An alien vessel crashes"—not 👎 "An alien vessel crash." If you have a singular subject (that is, just one alien vessel), you need to use a singular verb since that *agrees with* the subject. In the following examples, I italicize the simple subject of each sentence and boldface the verb:

👍 *Steam* **rises** from the crater created by one particular spaceship that crashed in the woods near their house.

Verb forms vary. Here, for example, is how the verb "to be" changes depending on whether the subject is *I, you* (singular), *he, she, it, we, you* (plural), or *they*:

To be (present tense)	Singular	Plural
First person	I **am**	we **are**
Second person	You (singular) **are**	you (plural) **are**
Third person	he/she/it **is**	they **are**
	Puneet **is**	She and Puneet **are**
	they **are**	

To be is an "irregular" verb in present tense since it has three forms that look quite different from one another (*is, are, am*). Most verbs have only two forms in the present tense, one ending with an *-s* and one without (*move/moves; run/runs; smile/smiles; enjoy/enjoys; create/creates*). The one ending in the *-s* is in the third-person singular.

👎 *It* **rise** from the ground and the ship itself. [Should be: *It* **rises** . . .]

👎 The enormous spaceship in the woods, though, **were** starting to disintegrate. [Should be **was**.]

Again—and this is crucial—the word indicating the principal actor—the "doer" or "experiencer" or "exister" of your sentence—determines the form of the verb that you should use. These following verb forms all *agree with* their subjects; in other words, they match up with them:

Doer:

👍 *Some citizens* **ran out** to purchase weapons.

Experiencer:

👍 The couple **felt** a weird mixture of fear, anxiety, and agitation.

Exister:

👍 The *spaceship* **was made** of a strange substance no one could identify.

Even in passive constructions,[3] you can locate the subject by determining who or what is the principal doer, experiencer, or exister that is the receiver of the action:

👍 When he was a child, *Puneet* **was stung** by a scorpion. His world **was changed** by that childhood trauma.

[True, it's the scorpion that acts (does the stinging), but Puneet is the subject because his name appears where it does in the sentence (at the head of the main clause).

---

[3] I give some examples of passive voice sentences in chapter 1 (p. 31) and discuss the passive voice in more detail in chapter 3, pages 80–84.

He is the experiencer that this passive sentence is focused on. If you want to put this in the active voice, that's not difficult: "A scorpion stung him when Puneet was just a child." This makes *scorpion* the subject, and the verb *stung* agrees with it.]

Subjects Both Plural and Singular

Sometimes a subject can work as either singular or plural. Your choice of verb form indicates which you have decided is the case. For example, in the following sentence, the subject could be either singular or plural:

👍 The *spaceships' landing and their widespread disintegration* **was/were** alarming.

Are you saying that the landing and disintegration = one event, a single totality? If so, then you should use *was*. If you want to emphasize the fact that the invasion and disintegration are two separate things, then you should use *were*. It's up to you; you have to decide what meaning you want to convey.

This resembles the situation in sentences like the following: "Four beers was too much for him" or "Two spoonfuls of honey is all I can stand." If you want to emphasize the totality of the four beers or the two spoonfuls of honey, then singular verb forms are fine. As with the previous sentence, a plural form in these situations would be acceptable but I think less effective. It's a close call, though.

Here is another example, this time of what's called a *collective noun*:

👍 The *state board* of security were/was undecided as to a course of action.

If you want to stress that every single member was undecided, use *were*; if the whole board as an entity was undecided, then *was* would be better. When dealing with collective nouns like the *state board*, or words like *family, staff, flock, faculty*, it's up to you to determine whether you want to convey singularity or plurality. Within a single piece of writing, though, it's best to be consistent; if you're using a plural with *faculty* in one place, you should use it elsewhere too. Usually, though not always, collective nouns take a singular verb in US English.

Collective nouns are words for single units that are composed of many different entities or members, like *family, board of trustees, company, regiment, army, pack, herd*. It is interesting to note the variety of collective nouns used in reference to animals: a *shrewdness* of apes; a *cloud* of bats, a *sleuth* of bears, a *quiver* of cobras, a *mischief* of mice, a *smuck* of jellyfish, a *pride* of lions, a *murder* of crows. (There are many others, but those are my favorites.)

Some words in English sound plural, too, but take a singular verb.

👍 In general, the *news* was not good.

👎 The news *were* not good. [This is an understandable error, but *news* is singular.]

Athletics, scissors, gallows, physics, mathematics, economics, and many names of other academic disciplines fall into this same category, as do some illnesses (like the *measles*). You can identify them by taking the *s* off the end. If the word remaining is not a noun (or even a word), you have one of these plural-sounding singular nouns.

Subject Dictates Verb Form

I mention earlier that the subject determines the verb. This might seem counterintuitive when all the words following the verb seem to disagree with the verb form you picked, but that disagreement, while awkward, is acceptable:

👍 The most pressing *problem* **is** the three spaceships in the schoolyard. ["Problem" is singular, so the verb is singular even though "the three spaceships" is plural.]

👎 The most pressing *problem* **are** the three spaceships in the schoolyard. ["Problem" is singular, so "are" does not work here.]

👍 The *three spaceships* in the schoolyard **are** the most pressing problem.

Prepositions and Subject-Verb Agreement

On occasion, a subject will seem to be plural but will still require a singular verb. This often occurs when a *prepositional phrase* intervenes between the subject and verb. Such a phrase consists of a preposition and a noun—a noun that's called the *object of the preposition*. Intervening prepositional phrases *do not* affect the form of verb. The subject determines the verb.

There are over a hundred common prepositions in English. The literary critic and poet William Empson eloquently describes them:

> The English prepositions . . . used in so many ways and in combination with so many verbs, have acquired not so much a number of meanings as a body of meaning continuous in several dimensions; a tool-like quality, at once thin, easy to the hand, and weighty, which a mere statement of their variety does not convey. (8)

> **Prepositions** are small connecting words like *as, about, above, across, after, against, along, among, around, as, before, behind, below, beneath, by, concerning, despite, down, during, except, for, from, in, into, like, near, of, off, on, onto, out, outside, over, through, toward, under, until, up, with, according to, along with, apart from, as for, because of, by means of, except for, in addition to, in case of, on top of, outside of,* and the like.
>
> A **prepositional phrase** consists of the preposition and the word or words immediately after it, and typically modifies or specifies the meaning of a noun or a verb (that is, it functions as an adjective or as an adverb).

They form an integral part of language and have significant linguistic power: they can provide locational data (*above, in, behind*), signify a possessive (*of*), indicate time information (*during, until*), and work in a variety of assorted linkages (many can be subordinators). Sometimes they even can have abstract or symbolic resonance (*beyond, before*).

Prepositions have been the subject of a longstanding and controversial prohibition: "Never end a sentence on a preposition!" This prohibition is simply misguided. It's fine to end a sentence on a preposition and often makes for a better sentence than one that's reordered to end on another word.

👍 "Alien spaceships in our backyard?" Puneet asked. "That's not something I ever dreamed of!"

Of course, Puneet could have ended with "imagined" rather than "dreamed of," but his sentence is acceptable as is.

To return to the issue of subject-verb agreement, prepositions intervening between subject and verb should be ignored
when deciding on the verb. For example, *as well as* or *in addition to* indicate something added to something else, but
they lack the pluralization power or connective capacity
(let's call it) of *and*:

👍 The populace as well as the president **was** alarmed.
[Subject, **populace**, is singular.]

👎 Arpita as well as her husband Puneet **were** spending
longer and longer periods enMeshed, trying to gather
information. [Should be **was** spending.]

👍 Arpita and Puneet **were working** harder than they
ever had. [Subject is plural.]

As well as does indeed suggest addition. So why doesn't it
function the same way as *and*? I think the explanation is that
the preposition introduces only a parenthetical element and
hence does not affect the subject. In the following pair of sentences, the first includes a parenthetical element, which has
no impact on the verb; the second, without the parentheses,
requires a plural verb form:

👍 The alien *spaceship* in his backyard (and the thousands of others all over the world) **was** timed to open
at noon, Greenwich Mean Time.

👍 The alien *spaceship in his backyard and the thousands
of others all over the world* **were** timed to open at noon
Greenwich Mean Time.

Subject Sometimes Divided into Two Parts

In some sentences, the subject and verb are split into two parts. Called **correlative constructions**, such sentences use a structure of "Both ... and," "Either ... or," "Neither ... nor," or "Not only ... but also." The subjects can be singular or plural. Occasionally one subject is singular and the other plural—in which case the verb needs to agree with the part of the subject closest to it.

👍 Neither *President Akbaliatuk* nor the *legislators* **were** able to help.

👍 Neither the *legislators* nor the *president* **was** able to help.

👍 Not only *earth* but also *Venus, Mars, and Jupiter* **were** invaded.

👍 Not only *Venus, Mars, and Jupiter,* but also *earth* **was** invaded.

Constructions such as these appear more often in academic writing than in fiction or in writing intended for a general public.

Verbs Can Sometimes Precede Subjects

Sometimes English sentences do not start with the subject, and thus you need to anticipate whether that subject will be plural or singular. You need to think ahead a bit. The most typical situation is one in which you start with "There is" or "There are," with *there* functioning as what's sometimes called a "dummy subject":

👍 There is *panic* in many parts of the world.

👍 There are *crowds and riots* all over.

👎 There's *many worried people* out there. [Should be: There **are** many worried people out there.]

Sometimes, though, with a compound subject, a sentence such as the following is acceptable:

👍 There is *great unrest, worry, and fear* all across the globe.

Unrest, worry, and fear here constitute a singular entity, so *there is* works. *There are* would be acceptable (👍👎), but less than ideal, I think, since it would sort of de-link the words "unrest," "fear," and "worry."

Like fragments and run-ons, subject-verb errors will significantly undermine your status as a credible, reliable voice. Making sure your subjects and verbs agree has the effect of reminding your reader what the sentence is actually about—namely, who or what the doer, experiencer, or exister is—and emphasizing that entity's singular or plural status.

PART TWO
Communicativeness

Writing strives to communicate. You're trying to get across an idea to a certain audience, and you want to make sure that it understands exactly what you mean.

The sentence, the basic element of written communication, establishes a humble beginning, a simple starting point. Within the sentence, the subject and the (tensed) verb provide the essence of your message. All sentences consist of "a noun that's verbing." If you've read this far, you know what a noun is. But what does "verbing" involve?

Verbs take many different forms. Table 1 attempts to provide an overview, dividing tenses into past, present, and future, and variants of these. Using these forms in the right places will greatly increase your language's effectiveness at conveying what you intend.

Table 1. Verb Tenses: The Essentials

	Present	Past	Future
Simple	Happens right now or on a regular basis.	Happened at a particular point or over a period of time.	Will happen.
	*Arpita **enjoys** life.*	*The aliens **landed**.*	*Arpita **will enjoy** life.*
	*The moon **rises** every night.*	*Arpita **enjoyed** life.*	
Perfective aspect[a]	Started in past, continues into present (or stops at present moment).	Started in past, completed in past, prior to something else taking place.	Starts in past, present, or future, and completed in future.
	*Puneet **has enjoyed** life (up until now).*	*Puneet **had enjoyed** life.*	*Puneet **will have enjoyed** life.*
Progressive aspect	Present continuous, ongoing (brief) action.	Past continuous action, brief or now ended.	Future continuous action not yet started.
	*He **is living** life to its fullest.*	*He **was enjoying** life.*	*He **will be savoring** a life well lived.*
Perfective progressive aspect	Started in past, continues in present.	Started in past, ends in past, prior to some other occurrence.	Started in past, will continue in future for indefinite period.
	*Arpita and Puneet **have been writing** for a long time now.*	*He **had been planning** an ordinary life before the alien invasion took place.*	*By 2035, they **will have been writing** for over a decade.*

Modal[b] + verb (Note: verb can be omitted if it's understood.)	Possible/probable/obligative: present sense of an imagined, possible, or wished-for past.	Similar to other modal: present sense of an imagined, possible, or wished-for present or future.
	Modal + have + past participle.	Modal + infinitive (minus the "to").
	Modal + have been + past or present participle, adjective, or noun phrase.	Modal + be + past or present participle, adjective, or noun phrase.
	*I **should have tried**.*	*I **should/could/would try**.*
	*I **might have been writing** that article.* *It **could've been** a mess.*	*I **should be writing** that article.* *I **might be** sad.* *I **could be** a father.*

[a] Some authors (for example, Behrens) prefer to call these tenses; they are variations or **aspects** of the basic tenses.

[b] Modals include the following: ***should, could, would, might, may, must, ought, can***. The modal ***will*** helps to create the future tense. Modals are not used with ***has*** or ***had*** (⚐ I might had . . .) and are not doubled (⚐ You can should try).

3

Verbs

In English, the verbs are quite complicated. The language has many tenses, and verb forms are used in a host of complex ways to convey a wide range of meanings. People talk about the *tense* of a verb, its *aspect*, its *mood*, and its *voice*, all of which I will touch on in this chapter. But I should start by offering a definition of the base form of the verb, the *infinitive*.

The base form of a verb is called an **infinitive**, which usually includes the "infinitive marker" *to*: *to go*, *to decide*, *to run*. The various verb tenses and forms are created out of this infinitive: *I go*, *she goes*, *they go*; *I decide*, *he decides*; *I run*, *Puneet runs*. Note that *to be* is the only infinitive form that does not appear in its present tense in formal English. (It does appear in several dialects of English, however: "I be trying to deal with this AQI issue"). An infinitive can function as a noun or as a modifier (adverb or adjective). "*To love* is *to live*" (nouns); "In his youth, Puneet wanted *to excel*" (adverb); "The invasion was ultimately something *to embrace*" (adjective).

Basic Tenses: Review

As previously mentioned, the three basic tenses are *present tense*, indicating something that is happening or going on right now; the *past tense*, which indicates something was ongoing or already took place—could be thirty seconds or a billion years ago; and the *future tense*, which indicates something has not yet taken place, something that will happen, or that is going to occur. Here are some more examples of the basic tenses:

Present:

👍 Puneet dislikes the nail-mons and their effect on his life.

Past:

👍 Like almost everyone else, the couple **lived** a relatively normal life prior to the implantation of nail-mons.

Future:

👍 They **will see** how these biometric and enMeshing devices change their lives in the coming years.

Shall can also be used to designate obligation, especially in formal documents that make declarations such as,

👍 It is resolved that all artifacts found near the alien vessels **shall be brought** to the proper authorities and that those who fail to do so **shall be held** in violation of local and federal laws.

Such a usage is slightly ambiguous since it's often unclear whether the *shall* expresses a *should* or a simple *will*.

Shall also occurs in certain questions, such as, "*Shall* we dance?" Note that this has a slightly different meaning from "*Will* we dance?" the "*shall*" offering an invitation to a near-future activity, and the "*will*" a future speculation.

In general, though, both forms denote futurity. "*Shall*" (and "*shan't*," contracted form of "*shall not*") has a legalistic and slightly old-fashioned ring to it, at least in the United States. On the other hand, the British seem to favor retaining "*shall*," especially in first-person sentences.

Perfect Tenses (or the Perfective Aspect)

As you almost certainly know, there are additional verb forms, ones that add relevance and complexity to your sentences. **Perfective forms** include the following: *present perfect*, *past perfect* (sometimes called *pluperfect*), and *future perfect*.

Present perfect shows action or experience that started in the past and (here is the "relevance") is either still going on or has just ended.

- 👍 Like many others, Puneet and Arpita **have felt terrified** ever since the landing. [Started in past, still going on.]

- 👍 The aliens **have begun** to emerge from their spaceships. [Started in past, still going on.]

- 👍 Now it seems as though all the alien spaceships **have landed**. [Action in past that just ended.]

- 👍 The president **has spoken** about the invasion and **has assured** us that there is no danger. [Action in past that has just ended.]

Helping words (or auxiliary words) include *has, had, have,* as well as words such as *is, are, be,* and *were*. These words often precede the participle and provide information about when something happened, when it started or ended, and if it is still happening. These words help form what are commonly called the **perfect** tenses, such as present perfect—*has* eaten, *have* run; past perfect—*had* lived; future perfect—*will have* understood. They also help form the **continuous** or **progressive** tenses—*is helping, was struggling, will be writing*. In addition, there are also **perfect progressive** tenses: *has been helping, had been struggling, will have been writing*.

Sometimes these grammatical formations are called the perfective and progressive **aspects** of the verb, **aspect** being "a grammatical feature of verbs and auxiliaries relating to completion, duration, and repetition" (Kolln et al., 337). Note too that **aspect** provides "current relevance," going beyond indication of whether something merely takes place in the past, present, or future (see Nelson 124).

Past perfect denotes something that took place in the past and (the "current relevance") also ended in the past:

- 👍 Initially, the president initially **had declared** that the landings were an elaborate hoax. He was wrong.

- 👍 Prior to the invasion, Puneet and Arpita **had been** content, confident that their future was bright.

- 👍 Initially many people **had thought** our country was being invaded by a hostile superpower.

The past perfect gives a clear endpoint to an action that was started in the past. Very often (as in the three preceding examples), the tense indicates a sharp change in direction or expectation.

Future perfect deals with an action that started in the past, is starting in the present, or that will start in the future—and will come to an end in the future, all of which temporal issues are quite "relevant" to the meaning conveyed.

👍 Assuming that the planet still exists, next month Puneet and Arpita **will have been** married twenty years. [Started in past, has an endpoint (twenty years of marriage) in the future.]

👍 Even if the aliens all leave tomorrow, they **will have made** a permanent mark on history. [Will start in future, will end in the future.]

Progressive Tenses (or the Progressive Aspect)

Verbs also exist in what are traditionally called the **progressive** or **continuous** forms. This is also sometimes referred to as the **progressive aspect** of a verb and indicates an action that is ongoing (continuous) by using an *-ing* participial form (present participle).

Present progressive shows action taking place at the present moment, adding some relevance to the time indication by stressing that it is continuous but not long-lasting:

👍 EnMeshed, their hands curled up, holograms dancing in the air before them, many people **are ignoring** all that's happening around them. [Simple present, **ignore**, seems to imply a general listlessness; the progressive aspect suggests an active, intentional ignoring of what's happening.]

👍 Arpita and Puneet **are planning** to stay put, however. [Again, the continuous form emphasizes ongoing activity that has current relevance.]

The **past progressive** shows action that took place over a limited time period in the past. Note how these aspects give a very different meaning from simple past tense:

👍 Their newspaper **was preparing** a special issue on the American Dream. This was put on hold, however. [This sentence shows how an ongoing action was interrupted prior to completion.]

👍 The newspaper **prepared** a special issue on the American dream. [Past tense.]

👍 Many citizens **were doing** all they could to acquire weaponry. [There is an active quality to the citizens' actions.]

👍 Many citizens **did** all they could to acquire weaponry. [Past tense makes the citizens' actions sound slightly desperate.]

Future progressive describes action in the future that typically will take place over an extended period:

👍 Politicians **will be campaigning** on the basis of how effectively they responded to the aliens. [Compare **will campaign**, which seems at once less active and more neutral.]

👍 Many previously chilly international relations **will be thawing** as countries join forces to respond to the invasion. [Compare **will thaw**, which suggests something that will happen definitely and very swiftly.]

Present perfect progressive shows something that started in the past and continues until now and perhaps beyond:

👍 For a long time, Puneet **has been studying** astronomy in an attempt to discern if and where other intelligent life exists in the galaxy.

👍 The populace at large **has been adapting** to all kinds of incredible changes in the world.

Past perfect progressive shows action that started in the past but has just ended. That is, something happened to halt it, or it just stopped. The aspect implies a reversal of a previous state of affairs.

👍 For a long time, Puneet **had been longing** for proof that there were other sentient entities in the universe.

👍 Arpita, meanwhile, **had been hoping** for a slow news day so that her piece on the American Dream (from the perspective of an immigrant) would capture a lot of attention.

Future perfect progressive shows action that, continuous and ongoing, will be completed in the future:

👍 If they last till the summer, the couple **will have been writing and reporting** for ten years.

Since aspect adds specificity and suggests relevance, choosing the right aspect is as important a communicative decision as choosing the right tense.

Modals

Modals are additional auxiliary or helping words that combine with verb forms, usually suggesting possibility, probability, or obligation. They include the following: *may, might, must, could, can, would,* or *should.* These differ from the auxiliaries formed from *to be* and *to have,* though, since they can't stand on their own as the verb of a sentence (for example, no one says, "I could this" or "he might that," but they might say, "I could understand," or "he might help"). Modals offer the present view of a likely, wished-for, or possible past, present, or future state. They add subtle shades of meaning and precision to your writing.

Here are some examples of modals used to give a present view of a probable, possible, or wished-for past:

- 👍 The president **should have done** more in the early stages of the invasion. [modal + have + past participle]

- 👍 As a journalist, Puneet felt that he **might have worked** more diligently to calm the public's fears. [modal + have + past participle]

- 👍 Arpita realized she **could have been writing** more relevant articles. [modal + have been + present participle]

- 👍 The president realized it **would have been** a total political disaster if he had followed his party's suggestion to quarantine women, children, and the elderly in detainment camps. [modal + have been + noun phrase]

- 👍 In general, the populace **might have been** happier if the aliens were not so strange and numerous. [modal + have been + adjective]

The following examples show how modals can sometimes offer a present view about a possible, probable, or wished-for present or future:

Possible present:

   👍 Most people felt they **should be** afraid but were not. [modal + infinitive (without *to*) + adjective]

   👍 Like many others, their next-door neighbor **could be** counted on to blame the nail-mons and the Mesh for the alien invasion. [modal + infinitive (without *to*) + past participle]

Possible future:

   👍 Puneet **should be** getting nail-mons installed on his toes fairly soon. These gave about fifty additional biometrics. [modal + infinitive (without *to*) + present participle]

   👍 There was widespread concern that many humans **might crack** under the strain. [modal + infinitive (without *to*)]

Wished-for future:

   👍 Secretary of State Miguel Corderas declared, perhaps prematurely, that everyone **should open their homes** in friendship to the aliens. [modal + infinitive (without *to*)]

   👍 Arpita thought she **should write** a feature piece on how, without any direct communication, the aliens are inadvertently revealing people's hidden fears and true selves. [modal + infinitive (without *to*)]

Common Problems of Modal Use

Modals do not combine with *has* or *had*, nor are they typically doubled:

🖓 He **should had** realized the problem. [The correct form is *should have*.]

🖓 "I **might could** make a big difference," their neighbor Garrastazu declared, a sinister look in his eye. [This is slang; use either modal by itself.]

🖓 In his living room, Garrastazu's TV was on, and someone from an old cowboy movie was saying, "You shouldn't a-oughta a-done that." [This slang line is the contracted form of "you should not have ought to have done that," which is also clearly nonstandard. The correct version would be, "You shouldn't have done that," or "You oughtn't to have done that," which are formal English but far less memorable.]

You should also note in these preceding examples the correct spelling of the verbs: you need to make sure that you spell out the *have* in *should have, could have, would have,* and similar constructions. If you want the contracted forms, though, they are *should've, could've, would've.* Often these verb forms incorrectly appear in writing as *should of, could of, would of* (or as *shoulda, coulda, woulda*).

🖓 The president **could of** resigned during the crisis. [Should be **could have** or **could've**.]

🖓 Puneet and Arpita **shoulda** known that as reporters of the news they were going to have to take risks, even in remote American towns. [**Shoulda** should be **should have** or **should've**.]

Here are two frequently confused verb forms that often emerge with these more complex tenses:

☞ In the midst of trying to run down what was happening elsewhere on the planet, Puneet said, "I **should have went** to law school." [Should be **should have gone**.]

👍 Arpita said, "Yeah, and then you **would have gone** crazy."

☞ Garrastazu suddenly appeared at their door and said, "I **seen** what you wrote in the newspaper, and I don't like it." [This is colloquial speech and understandable, but **I have seen** or **I saw** are the formal written English versions.]

Two Other Ways to Represent Tense: Phrasal Modals

Phrasal modals are groups of words that indicate tense and that always combine with an infinitive form. Larsen-Freeman and Celce-Murcia provide a useful list of these phrases, linking them to the one-word modal forms they're relatively synonymous with.[1] These phrasal forms are used very often, especially in speech.

---

[1]   Here is their list of typical modals and the phrasal modals they can generate (139):

can, could→be able to
will, shall→be going to, be about to, be to
must→have to, have got to, need to
should→be supposed to
would (for past habit)→used to
may, might→be allowed to, be permitted to

   As you can see, this list is not exhaustive, but it provides an excellent starting point.

For example, "used to" suggests that something was typically or habitually done, and over a longish time period, in the past, but is done no more.

👍 Puneet used to be more patient with his neighbor, but Garrastazu's behavior had become too threatening.

Note that this is frequently rendered incorrectly as *use to*, perhaps because the *d* is silent. But when you use this expression in writing, you want to preserve the *d*, except in constructions such as the second example, where the final *d* is sometimes dropped:

👎 Arpita use to look forward to going to work every day. [Should be *used*.]

👎 👍"Garrastazu didn't use to be so bad, did he?" Puneet asked Arpita.

👍 "No," she replied, "He never used to be so weird. I guess the aliens bring out the worst in some people."

Another phrasal modal that causes some issues is "going to." This indicates futurity, perhaps with a little more of a sense of intentionality or determination than the simple future:

👍 "If he continues acting this way," Puneet went on, "I'm going to report him to the authorities."

👎 "I think you're gonna find they're pretty busy elsewhere," Arpita replied. [*Gonna* is the nonstandard form of *going to*.]

Sometimes these phrasal modals can be combined:

👍 "I'm going to need to be able to get their attention, I guess, maybe via an opinion piece in the paper,"

> Puneet mused. [This strings together three phrasal
> modals, which seems to be the limit (S. Weigle,
> quoted by Larsen-Freeman and Celce-Murcia.[2])]

Word-processing programs often will highlight phrasal
modals as being too wordy, but it seems to me that they often
provide useful variations of simple modal forms.

Mood: In Particular, the Subjunctive

Verb mood or mode is important, too. It represents the at-
titude of the speaker or writer toward their sentence's
meaning or intended purpose. For example, the indicative
mood offers simple factual material—past, present, or future. The imperative mood gives a command: "Do not
attack the alien visitors!" The interrogative mood asks a
question; the exclamatory mood exclaims: "How nice that
these aliens are so serene!" or "What a scary world this is!"
There are several others, the most important of which is the
subjunctive.

Occasionally, you will want to say something that you
know is "contrary to fact" or speculative in nature, and you
need to use a different mood altogether. You are not trying to
deceive anyone. You are just offering a kind of "what if." In
these situations, the *subjunctive* mood is used for the verb,
typically *were*, or in the perfect form, *had been*:

🖒 Puneet: If I was president now, I'd do something.

🖒 Arpita: You mean "if I **were** president."

---

[2]   I believe that S. Weigle is Sara Cushing, professor of linguistics at Georgia
State University.

👍 Puneet: Oh, right. We need a woman president.
   If I **were** a woman, I'd run.

When should you use *were*, which is what Arpita insists that Puneet use? Benjamin Dreyer has developed a helpful test:

> If you're writing of a situation that is not merely not the case, but is unlikely, improbable, or just plain impossible, you can certainly reach for a "were." . . .
>
> If you're writing of a situation that is simply not the case but could be, you might opt for a *was*. . . .
>
> Also, if you're acknowledging some action or state of being that most certainly did occur—that is, if by "if" what you really mean is "in that"—you want a "was." (101)

The first instance Dreyer cites is precisely what Puneet is doing when he says, "If I were president." He's not president and has no political aspirations. An example of the second instance, where we have a somewhat counterfactual but possible situation, might be this:

👍 Puneet said, "If I **was** able to find the fountain pen I lost last week, I'd be able to record some good ideas."

The third instance might be exemplified with this sentence:

👍 "If I **was** annoyed last night about your nail-mons, I chalk it up to stress. Please forgive me," Puneet said. [No subjunctive needed—this is just past tense.]

Past possibilities or counterfactuals (contrary-to-fact situations) use the perfect subjunctive, which is the same as the past perfect tense (*had* plus past participle):

👎 If the country **was** better prepared and better educated about the possibility of alien encounters, there would be less automatic fear of invaders. [This should be "if the country **had been** better prepared."]

There's a second, slightly more obscure use of the subjunctive mood. It occurs in present-tense sentences with a *that*-clause, where a command, suggestion, proposal, requirement, recommendation, or similar order or piece of advice is made. I think of these constructions (called *mandative* sentences) as ones that include an invisible but implicit *should* or *must*. Here are some examples. I have boldfaced the subjunctive mood verb and italicized the words signaling the need for the subjunctive:

👍 Authorities now *recommend that* all citizens **be** mindful of the current situation.

👍 State law *requires that* the mayor **report** any unusual circumstances.

👍 "I *recommend that* everyone **monitor** these invading vessels," the president said, "and I *suggest that* each American citizen **display** patience with our alien visitors."

Note that the three previous sentences use the infinitive forms (without *to*) of the verbs *to be, to report, to monitor*, and *to display*, and that the constructions could be seen as having a silent or implicit modal like *should* or *must*.

The subjunctive is also required after sentences in which adjectives such as the following are used: *crucial, necessary, advisable, proper, urgent, fitting, obligatory, vital, essential*. Again an implicit but unstated modal such as *should* precedes the subjunctive mood verb forms in the following sentences:

👍 Puneet wrote, "It is *essential that* each individual **learn** as much as possible about the aliens."

👍 He further declared, "It is *advisable* that people **be** cautious using any weapons against the invaders, who are in fact quite peaceful."

While the subjunctive is being used less and less, it improves communicativeness, either reinforcing the counterfactual aspect of a contrary-to-fact situation or offering a soft command, thus bolstering a mandate, principle, or necessity. Its correct use also enhances your credibility with certain audiences. Note too that while it might seem to be falling out of favor, it is used in many situations that sound so normal to us that we don't realize the subjunctive mood is being employed: "If it please the court," "as it were," and "if need be" are some examples.

Voice: Passive versus Active

As I mention earlier (pages 31 and 55), in the passive, the subject receives the action. The active voice is the opposite: the subject performs the action (or does the existing). The passive is formed by using *to be* verbs, usually *was*, *were*, or *had been*, and putting the main verb into its past participle form. This construction moves offstage—ignores—the agent that performed the action of the sentence. The active "The president concealed the information," for example, thus becomes in passive, "The information was concealed." English teachers, editors, and even word-processing programs generally recommend that the active voice be employed since it clearly states who did what and to whom.

The problem is that the passive voice has a shiftiness, a deceptiveness built in. Passive constructions offer what some linguists call "agent delete"; the agent performing the action does not appear in the sentence's information. "It was decided that the newspaper lay off 30 percent of its employees" leaves out the crucial information of who decided this, and when, and why. The passive voice suffuses bureaucratese; it's a staple of corporate-speak. It often falsifies via omission. A famous example, "Mistakes were made," blames no one, offers no responsibility.[3]

Sometimes I ask students to "passivize" sentences, just to see how this affects meaning. For example, "Would-be insurrectionists invaded the US Capitol on January 6, 2021," differs from "The US Capitol was invaded by would-be insurrectionists on January 6, 2021." In the passive version, placing "The US Capitol" first thrusts the whole sentence into a historical light; it drains the event of its immediacy and at the same time diminishes the shocking actions of the "would-be insurrectionists." Similarly, telling someone who has just come back from a long illness, "You were very much missed," differs quite a lot from saying, "I missed you very much," or even "We missed you very much." The active voice, which the latter two sentences employ, is not just more direct but also more personal; it compassionately proclaims friendliness. The passive, by contrast, has a remote, distancing effect,

---

[3]   The title and subtitle of Carol Tavris and Elliot Aronson's book captures the essence of the problem with the passive: *Mistakes Were Made (But Not by Me): Why We Justify Foolish Beliefs, Bad Decisions, and Hurtful Acts* (Brilliance Audio, 2014).

casting the agents who missed the person as existing long ago and far away.

On the other hand, many academic fields, especially in the sciences, require the passive. Its use denotes detached objectivity. Such objectivity also comes into play in journalism. If you are a journalist writing about a crime, say, you need to be careful you don't slander someone who should be assumed innocent until proven guilty. In that case, the passive is the right voice to use:

- 👍 Directly after the invasion, the local population looted the stores, reporters observed. [This sentence in active voice more or less convicts "the local population."]

- 👍 It was reported that, directly after the invasion, stores were looted. [Passive is not accusing anyone of anything.]

Usually, though, such indirectness is not a virtue. Keep in mind that if and when you resort to the passive, you inevitably suppress vital elements of the situation. Saying, "The car was hit," suggests that no one had anything to do with it; the car just "got hit"—who knows who hit it, when, or even what the situation was. Here's what is happening in our narrative:

- 👍 A nail-mons-distracted driver who was tailgating Arpita rear-ended her when she slowed for a yield sign.

What happened after the accident? Who was at fault? The next sentence shows how the passive can be so vague as to be deceptive:

- 👎 Neither driver was ticketed by the police. The driver of the car that Arpita's car was struck by said her vision was briefly obstructed.

The fact that the police chose not to issue tickets suggests no one was at fault. Furthermore, the driver also appears to have been victim of some outside, interfering element.

Putting this in the active voice and adding some agents sheds a different light on the matter:

👍 After they arrived, police did not ticket either driver. The driver of the car that struck Arpita's said that an insect or piece of dust flew into her eye and briefly obstructed her vision.

In the active voice, the whole situation seems very different: the police seem possibly negligent, and the driver of the car that hit Arpita sounds like she's making up the bug-in-the-eye story. (She was on her nail-mons, no doubt.) The passive concealed such information.

When you use the passive, you might ask yourself if you are trying to hide anything and then cast the sentence in the active voice, which is almost always preferable. Here are two more examples:

👎 After an investigation, it was determined that no one was at fault. [Passive.]

👍 After an investigation, the insurance company determined no one was at fault. [Active.]

The first sentence makes it seem as though the "no fault" decision was correct and obvious: "it was determined" sounds very authoritative. But moving the same idea to the active voice changes things: of course the insurance company will opt for whatever costs them less money.

The passive voice expresses vague imprecision. At the same time it seems to offer a state of affairs that's fixed, decided upon, and final, almost historically inevitable—but often a deceptively flat, agent-less recounting of events. Your choice of voice—active or passive—subtly slants the information that you're providing, or that is being provided to you.

On the Overuse of *To Be* Verbs

Many teachers and editors discourage the use of a large number of *to be* verbs—namely, *am, is, are, were, was, be, been, being*. The recommendation has some merit: these verbs tend to be weak (not active enough, often in passive voice) and often demonstrate "padding" on the writer's part. I would advise you to monitor your use of *to be* verbs: when you use more than one in a single sentence, or when you find that every sentence you write contains such verbs, consider rephrasing:

☞ The trouble with the invasion *was* that most citizens *were* confused about what actually *was* happening, and the authorities *were* unwilling to reveal what *was* proven *to be* true.

To rephrase . . .

👍 No one knew anything about the invasion, and the authorities refused to comment.

Half the length of the first, the second sentence captures most of its meaning of its wordier variant—and does so with more force and directness.

Infinitive "Splitting" Not a Problem

You might have heard of the rule prohibiting "split infinitives." Some people label as defective or substandard any sentence where a word is inserted between the *to* and the base form of the verb (in the following examples, *remedy* and *go*):

👍 Puneet and Arpita sought **to swiftly remedy** their fear. [Some insist that "to remedy swiftly" is preferable, but it seems to me that such a word order would be confusing.]

👍 They realized that, basically, their mission was **to boldly go** where no one has gone before, at least in a figurative sense. [This comes from the original *Star Trek*'s opening voiceover. Some people contend the sentence would be stronger with the word order "to go boldly," but the sentence has become so iconic that it's hard to say.]

Splitting infinitives does not indicate that a writer lacks literacy skills, nor does it undermine the authoritativeness of a piece of writing. If a sentence captures your meaning better with the split, leave it. In fact, sometimes a split infinitive is preferable to a version of the verb that keeps the *to* and the base form of the verb side by side.[4]

---

[4] Huddleston and Pullum, astute as usual, note that at times *not* splitting the infinitive reduces clarity, introducing an ambiguity or confusion (581).

4

Nouns and Pronouns

The linguist John Robert Ross contends that the noun—the word for a person, place, or thing—is the "coldest" of the parts of speech, all of which he envisions as existing on a "quasi-continuum." From hot to cold, we have verbs, participles, adjectives, prepositions, nouns. Ross writes,

> Proceeding along the hierarchy is like descending into lower and lower temperatures, where the cold freezes up the productivity of syntactic rules, until at last nouns, the ultimate zero of this space, are reached. (317)

Ross contends here that nouns have an emotional iciness, an inert remoteness. They are just the things of the world, bereft of adornment or vividness. By contrast, verbs can be marshaled to serve as other parts of speech and have many tenses and forms. Nouns can only be either singular or plural, possessive or nonpossessive. They form solid if inert stanchions in an uncertain sea, like the pilasters supporting a bridge.

Of course, some are more vibrant than others: *heart* and *lust* have more resonance than, say, *rock* or *dirt*. But contrasting those four nouns with their adjectival forms (*heartfelt, lusty, rocky*, and *dirty*) reveals the "cold" detachment of noun forms. For the most part, we rely on the words surrounding the nouns to provide warmth, specificity, and richness.

Still, although nouns often seem frozen in space and time, they form part of the necessary structure that writers build on when trying to communicate an idea. In this chapter, I want to examine various ways of using nouns—ways that are perhaps less icy than Ross might admit.

Gerunds or Gerund-Participles

Almost any noun can be made into a verb. In addition, verbs can be made into nouns. For example, you can take two verbs whose infinitive forms are *to run* and *to live* and put them into *-ing* forms: *running* and *living*. These words are usually used as verbs or adjectives, but they can also function as nouns:

👍 Running is living.

Nouns made out of verbs are called *gerunds* or *gerund-participles*, noun forms that seem reasonably active, or at least warmish.

When the infinitive form of the verb substitutes for the gerund, the result sounds slightly more formal and "cold":

👍 To run is to live.

Appositives

Noun vitality emerges also when nouns function as modifiers, or words that explain something about other nouns. Most modification in English is done through the use of adjectives and adverbs (or by prepositional phrases, functioning as adjectives or adverbs). Nouns, too, can modify even as they retain

If a noun or pronoun comes before a gerund, that noun or pronoun—unless it seems to have the force of a verb—needs to be in a possessive form, which connects the noun or pronoun to a person:

👍 Puneet did not approve of his wife's enMeshings, which were almost constant.

👍 👎 Glued to their televisions, millions of people watched the alien spaceship landing on the White House lawn. [Here, *landing* has the force of a verb, but some would contend that it is more formally correct to say *alien spaceship's landing*.[1]]

👎 Him longing to get back to normal life was acute. [Should be *His* longing.]

👎 Arpita and Puneet writing about the situation, though, helped them deal with it. [Should be *Arpita's and Puneet's*.]

If you follow the possessive-prior-to-a-gerund rule, it not only reinforces the impression that you are a careful writer or speaker, but it might even lend a little more warmth to your prose.

their noun-like character. They do this when they are used as *appositives*. The linguist Gerard M. Dalgish calls such modification "nonassertive equivalence."

---

[1]   Garner's example is better. He offers this exchange: "Is he singing?" "Yes, I heard him singing." "Is he talented?" "Yes, I heard his singing" (420).

Appositives reiterate or restate the noun, using different wording. Thus, in a sentence such as the following, *aliens* is immediately followed by another noun phrase, suggesting an equivalence without directly stating it. You can say that one noun is in **apposition to** the other. I will boldface the appositives in each of these:

👍 The aliens, **amorphous puddle-like beings that seemed more liquid than solid**, oozed their way into towns and villages.

👍 President Akbaliatuk, **our beleaguered and benighted leader**, spoke daily to our nation, **a collection of confused souls**.

In each case, a noun (*aliens, President Akbaliatuk, nation*) is reiterated using a different phrasing, one that "nonassertively" expands the scope and meaning of that noun. Using appositives can be an effective way to convey an idea subtly but honestly—and at the same time vivify your nouns.

Noun Clauses

Some clauses function the same way as a noun but contain a subject and verb themselves. I have highlighted here the noun (or nominal) clauses that function as subjects:

👍 **That the aliens were very strange** became immediately obvious.

👍 **People's wanting to touch them** became something of a problem.

👍 **What everyone longed for** was a clear explanation of events.

They can also function as objects:

👍 No one could figure out **which of the aliens was in charge**.

The **object** of a sentence is that noun, pronoun, or noun phrase that, in an active voice sentence, receives the action. It is "the thing acted on" (Garner 1017). It is also the word directly following a preposition, as in, "For **him**, the situation was especially worrisome." Note that pronouns, when in the object position, must be in the "objective" case: *me, you, him, him, her, us, them.*

Proper Nouns and Capitalization

Capitalization of proper nouns (names) can be surprisingly challenging. Sometimes a name will begin with a lowercase letter, as is the case with the baseball pitcher Jacob deGrom, the social critic bell hooks, or the poet e.e. cummings. If these lowercase names or initials begin a sentence, though, you need to capitalize the first letter. Every sentence needs to begin with a capital letter.

In general, use capital letters in the following situations:

- To begin a sentence.
- For names (proper nouns), unless people don't use capitals, as noted earlier.
- For names of countries, states, places, regions.
- For famous buildings, like the Capitol (note the spelling with the *o*).
- For time periods, like the Victorian Era.

- For most brand names unless they are lower case, like eKO yoga mats.

- For deities.

- For the first-person pronoun, I.

- For emphasis: DO NOT TAMPER WITH THE ALIEN SPACESHIPS! (In some styles, capitalization of whole words is in small capitals. In others, acronyms are in small capitals but capitalized whole words are in regular type.)

- For some acronyms, like AIDS, CPAP, NATO, COVID.

- For some initialisms: TNT, ESP, ALS, FBI, CIA.

- For first letters of words in titles of books/articles/stories/essays/plays. All words need to start with capital letters except prepositions, conjunctions, and articles. First and last words of titles always need to capitalized, though.

- For adjectives derived from names, like African or Ukrainian.

- Directions like *north*, *south*, *east*, and *west* are lowercase, unless you are using them in constructions like, "I lived in the Northwest for a decade."

- Seasons (winter, spring, summer, fall) are lowercase.

- In the complimentary close (or valediction) of a letter or e-mail, only the first word is capitalized: "Very truly yours," "All the best."

- For *Black*, when used in reference to a person's race. *Brown* and *White* (in reference to race) also may be capitalized for the sake of consistency.

Before you capitalize a word, you need to decide if there is a good reason to do so: is the word in some way special? Capital letters start a sentence; they occur in names of people, buildings, countries, brands; they're abbreviations; or they mark something unusual or distinctive about a word or a thing.

Pronouns: Three Issues

Pronouns, defined earlier (p. 30), are frequently a source of much confusion and controversy in written documents. The pronoun is a special type of noun, often substituting for another noun such as a proper noun (that is, for a name). You might wonder why I care so much about pronouns. They are just small words, and people almost always know what the writer means. I think of it this way: "Who Did What to Whom" inevitably matters. A lot. The idea, therefore, is to make it crystal-clear who or what the pronouns refer to.

Given that these words substitute for a previous word or group of words, you need to keep three issues in mind: *reference*, *agreement*, and *case*.

Pronoun Reference

First, is it obvious and evident to your reader which word preceding your pronoun is the one that your pronoun is subbing for?

Here is a problematic sentence that Puneet generates:

🖐 "The president and our editor are worried about how his power and position will be affected by the invasion."

👍 Arpita asked, "**His?**"

👍 Puneet replied, "The president's, of course."

The word or phrase that the pronoun replaces, called the **referent** or **antecedent**, needs to be clear and obvious to the reader, or else you're failing to communicate an important idea. In the sentence, "Arpita wondered if she had enough time to write a story," "Arpita" is the antecedent for the pronoun "she." "The president felt that his image and ratings were eroding," includes the pronoun "his," and it clearly refers to the antecedent "president." Fine.

On the other hand, if I were to start the paragraph you're now reading with, "This is a big issue," you might wonder what the pronoun "this" refers to, given that there are several possibilities. Put simply, whenever you use a pronoun, you need to make sure that your reader will recognize its antecedent, what it's substituting for. When there are multiple possible options, you can't leave your reader guessing.

It has to be instantaneously obvious which of the candidates for antecedent (among the preceding nouns) is the intended antecedent for your pronoun.

🖐 Arpita's mother and Puneet's mother were always in a struggle, and she always won. [Should be either "Arpita's mother always won" or "Puneet's mother always won."]

Sometimes antecedents are not needed. *I*, *my*, and other first-person pronouns do not require one. In sentences such as the following, no antecedent is needed for the pronoun *it*, which (like *there*), is often a "dummy subject":

👍 It was raining on the day after the aliens landed.

👍 It was annoying to have to rely so heavily on the Mesh, but everyone seemed to think it improved life.

But most pronouns require antecedents, and these need to be plain and obvious.

Pronoun Agreement

Second, does the pronoun *agree*, in terms of gender and number (plural or singular) with the noun it's replacing? If the antecedent is masculine, then the pronoun needs to be as well; if the antecedent is feminine, then the pronoun should be feminine. Similarly, a singular antecedent usually requires a singular pronoun, and a plural antecedent requires a plural pronoun.

👍 Puneet adjusted **his** tie. ["His" agrees with the gender of Puneet.]

👍 Arpita helped **him** adjust it. [This is OK since "him" agrees with the gender of Puneet.]

👍 She remarked, though, that she hated the color. ["She" refers to Arpita (from the previous sentence), and it works successfully here.]

Pronouns provide reinforcement as to whether the word they are standing in for is male or female (or neither) and whether it is singular or plural. Keep in mind, too, that many people now choose to be indicate their pronominal preference:

👍 This blogpost is authored by Arpita Tagore (she/her).

The Singular *They*: A Recent but Important Wrinkle

While a singular antecedent traditionally required a singular pronoun, *they* has come to be used also in reference to a singular antecedent when no gender is specified, as well as in reference to a singular antecedent that is nonbinary.

Thus, in the third-person singular, in addition to *he* and *she* and *it*, *they* can work. When referring to a singular antecedent, this is called the "singular *they*." This usage is controversial insofar as using a plural pronoun with a singular antecedent violates the principle of agreement, a key element of pronoun use.

For a long time, when no gender of the antecedent was specified, the default choice was the masculine pronoun. This was an example of how language rules aided and abetted the gender-biased idea that a male individual stood for or could represent humans of all genders.

Then, starting in the late 1970s or so, some editors, teachers, and writing handbooks recommended that pronouns be paired:

👎 👎 Each person should consult his/her own conscience about the best course of action he/she should follow.

Thankfully, the singular *they* has replaced that odd and awkward construction:

👍 Each person should consult their own conscience about the best course of action they should follow.

In addition, if you would prefer not to be categorized as either male or female (that is, as either *he* or *she*), you can use *they* (and *their*, *theirs*, *them*, *themself*) as your pronoun of choice. This variety of the singular *they* is called the "nonbinary *they*." You should use a plural verb with this, by the way:

👍 "Juanita, our managing editor, is at the door. They want to talk to you." [But not, "They wants to talk with you."]

The singular *they* was the American Dialect Society's "Word of the Year" in 2015. In 2020 it was declared their "Word of the Decade." The Modern Language Association (MLA) notes that the singular *they* "has emerged as a tool for making language more inclusive because it helps writers avoid making or enabling assumptions about gender" (Altreuter 92).

Pronoun Case

This brings me to the third pronoun issue: "case." Are you using the right type of the pronoun within your sentence? There are all kinds of pronouns, and they are not interchangeable. Each class, type, or "case" of pronoun presents its own difficulties and special features. Table 2 names these pronouns and gives brief descriptions of their use.

Subject Pronouns

Subject pronouns are used, as their name implies, as the subject of a sentence. These include the following: *I, you* (singular), *he/she/it/they*; *we, you* (plural), *they*.[1] Here are two subject pronouns:

👍 Arpita noted the aliens' resemblance to puddles. **She** realized, though, that **they** were definitely otherworldly entities.

To describe the sentence more fully and to offer a little more vocabulary, the *that* here introduces the *complement,* which can be a variety of parts of speech.

---

[1] Note that this and the subsequent pronoun lists will all follow the same pattern: first-, second-, third-person singular; then first-, second-, third-person plural.

A **complement** completes the meaning of the main verb, offering something akin to a repetition of the subject but using different wording (in the last half of the preceding example sentence, *they = otherworldly entities*). A complement is a sentence part that is offered as an equivalency, and it follows a *to be* or similar verb, called a *linking verb*. Others are *to seem*, *to become*, or many others in various circumstances. The complement can also be an **adjective**, as in "He was anxious" (*He = anxious*).

Traditionally, or conventionally, it's the subject pronoun that needs to follow *to be* verbs in constructions with a complement: "This is she." "It is I." "It is we."[2] I realize that this usage sounds a little awkward and strange, so you should reserve this usage for formal, written work. (A colleague of mine, though, said that if someone called him on the phone and asked for him, the best answer was "This is he," since it had the effect of intimidating most callers. "This is they" might be even more intimidating. But is intimidating callers the goal?[3])

Object Pronouns

Again, an object of the sentence is that which receives the action. Here are two sentences with direct objects (in boldface):

👍 Puneet slammed **the door**. Then he picked up **his empty glass**.

---

2   Following the infinitive, though, use the object form of the pronoun: "It was a good year to be him."

3   Perhaps.

Table 2. Pronoun Case

Case	Examples Enumerated	Use/Function
Subject	I, you, he, she, it, we, you, they	Function as subject of a sentence.
Object	me, you (singular), him, her, it, us, you (plural), them	Function as object of sentence or of a preposition.
Relative	that, which, where, when, who/whom	Introduce a relative (adjective) clause.
Possessive	1. my, your, his, her, its, our, your, their 2. mine, yours, his, hers, ours, yours, theirs	Indicate ownership or refer to an aspect of a thing or person. Group 1 pronouns occur with a noun; 2, without.
Interrogative	who, which, where, what, how	These introduce a question for which there could be a complex answer.
Indefinite	neither, either, someone, no one, everyone, both, all, somebody, nobody	Can function as subject or object; indefinite in their reference.
Indefinite relative	whoever, whenever, wherever, whatever	These have what might be termed a nonspecific reference.
Reflexive	myself, yourself, himself, herself, itself, ourself, ourselves, yourselves, themself, themselves	Emphasize a previous noun or pronoun; also show that doer and receiver of action are one and the same.
Demonstrative	this, that, these, those	Indicate something plural or singular, near or far; can be used as subject or object of sentence.

The following should be used with caution:

Anticipatory	usually subject pronouns	These occur prior to the referent.

Examples	Issues
She is tall. He is svelte.	Antecedent clarity and agreement. This case is used prior to *to be* verbs.
"Tell me," Arpita said. Puneet replied, "It's about us."	Often incorrectly used as subject: "Me and Puneet will write about it."
The aliens, which people feared and found exceptionally weird, did not try to communicate.	*Which* typically introduces nonessential elements; *that*, essential. *Whom* is falling out of speech.
Her idea, his plan, our problems, my dog; its nose, it was theirs.	Need to agree with antecedent; *their(s)* can be singular; no apostrophe needed to show possession.
"Which of the neighbors can we count on?" Arpita asked.	Note that these usually cannot work for a yes/no question.
Neither of them really understood what was going on. Either would do.	Except for *both* and *all*, take singular verbs. (Plural verbs sometimes better.)
Whatever they wrote seemed to cause controversy. Puneet said, "We need to be patient and kind." Garrastazu replied, "Whatever."	*Whatever* has taken on a meaning much larger than its definition implies; it indicates contempt or scorn for an inquiry or assertion.
They themselves were not afraid. They would work to uncover the truth. "I won't be able to do it myself, though!"	*Themself* and *ourself* are not standard, but their use is now accepted by most editors and teachers.
"This seems larger than those on the other side of the ridge," Puneet said about alien puddles.	*This* (near) and *that* (far) are singular; *these* (near) and *those* (far), plural. Often confused.
"They are up on the ridge, waiting and trigger-happy, those men with guns."	Their use is problematic—too often they distort the communication.

Kolln, Gray, and Salvatore give a good tip here: the direct object often is "the answer to a 'what' or 'whom' question" (45). What did Puneet slam? The door. What did he pick up? His empty glass.

An indirect object is a recipient or beneficiary of the verb's action; it's as if a *to* or *for* might be silently inserted. Here are two examples (indirect object in italics, direct in boldface):

👍 He handed *Arpita* **his empty glass**. "Was that Garrastazu again?" she asked.

👍 Puneet nodded. "I'm sending *the president* **an e-mail**," he said. "It should pop up on his nail-mons any second now."

Prepositions also have objects—namely, nouns or pronouns that receive the action. I have boldfaced these in the next sentences:

👍 When Garrastazu came to the door, Arpita smiled at **him**. Then she noticed his hands.

👍 "Why don't you have nail-mons, Garrastazu? For **me**, they're a lifeline."

👎 "Those darn things collect too much information for **them**, and they ain't getting any from **me**." [Unclear what the antecedent is of *them*. Off note, *ain't* is slang.]

Here are the object pronouns: *me, you, him/her/it/them; us, you, them*. These pronouns are often incorrectly used. Here is an example of a common pronoun-case error:

👎 "Me and Arpita were quite happy before the invasion," Puneet told people. [Should be "Arpita and I were quite happy . . ."]

In speech, using *me* as a subject ("Me and Arpita . . .") does get the idea across, but this usage also conveys, at least to some audiences, that either you do not know how to use pronouns or you're using an informal English. Some audiences will find that comforting and see you as an average Joe/Josephine, but others might find that particular usage annoying and juvenile, even in speech.

Pronoun case is often confused if more than one entity or person is the object of the preposition. In this situation, all the pronouns receiving action need to be objective case:

☞ Between he and Arpita a strong bond had formed over the years. [Should be "Between him and Arpita" or "Between Arpita and him."]

☞ Puneet said to Arpita, "I was just on the Mesh talking to our managing editor, and they are angry with you and I." [Should be "with you and me."]

☞ The managing editor said aloud, "He and Arpita I must see." [Should be "Him and Arpita."]

Note that in the last sentence ("Him and Arpita . . .") the object appears before the verb, but it still needs to be in objective case since it is receiving action. (This is an example of what's called *fronting*, where the object goes before the subject and verb. It's an unusual but acceptable construction.)

Possessive Pronouns

This group of pronouns includes **my**/*mine*; **your**/*yours*; **her**/*hers*; **his**/*his*; **their**/*theirs*; **its**/*its*; **our**/*ours*; **your**/*yours*; **their**/*theirs*. The boldfaced forms always occur before a noun; they are called "dependent" (*my* car, *her* article), while the italicized nonbolded forms are "independent" (The house is *ours*, the expression is *mine*) and are used when no noun follows.

Note that his, hers, yours, ours, theirs, and *its* end in an "s" and are possessive but do not require an apostrophe. The most frequently misused form is *its*, which is the dependent form of the possessive pronoun. *Its* always occurs before a noun.

> 🖓 The bear licked **it's** paws after having dipped them in an alien puddle. [Should be "its."]

> 🖓 After that, the look on **its'** face was amazing. [Should be "its." **Its'** is not a word.]

The independent form (no noun following), as in "The puddle was its," is not accepted by editors, grammarians, teachers, and linguists. There are better ways to capture the same idea. Still, I offer the possibility, in the second example sentence here:

> 👍 The alien near Puneet and Arpita's house made **its** [not **it's**] way across the driveway and slid under the garage door.

> 👍 🖓 The problems that alien encountered were **its** and **its** alone.

While this usage of *its* as an independent form is nonstandard, I give my example a thumbs-up/thumbs-down because science fiction allows considerable flexibility in terms of grammatical issues.

Reflexive Pronouns

These include *myself, yourself, himself/herself/itself/themself, ourselves, yourselves, themselves.* They suggest an emphasis of some kind.

👍 While many people were worried, Puneet **himself** was unafraid.

"Theirselves" is not acceptable in formal English. However, "themself" is now an acceptable reflexive form of the *singular they*.

Here is an example of the reflexive pronoun *themself* being used to refer to someone who is nonbinary or for whom *they* is their pronoun of choice:

👍 Puneet interviewed a person who prided **themself** on having made some physical contact with the aliens. They said it was a very strange experience.

Reflexive pronouns are also used when the doer and receiver of the action is the same.

👍 Arpita chided **herself** for not being more proactive since the invasion.

The plural form of *it* in reflexive is not *itselves* but *themselves*.

👍 The aliens somehow pulled **themselves** up the sides of buildings, slithering into windows and doors.

👍 Eurasia, the US, and several European countries have positioned **themselves** as antagonists of the alien invaders.

Note that reflexive case pronouns cannot be used as a subject or object in a sentence:

👎 "My nail-mons and myself have become one cyborgic entity," Puneet declared one day, apropos of nothing.

👍 Although she was enMeshed, Arpita looked over at her husband. "My nail-mons and *I*," she said. Puneet stared at her, then nodded. "Of course."

👎 "Give that delivery to Arpita or myself," Puneet said to the courier. [*Should be me,* not *myself.*]

Relative Pronouns

Relative pronouns include *who, whom, where, whose, that, which.* These introduce a *relative clause*, which functions as an adjective, modifying a noun or noun phrase.

👍 President Akbaliatuk, **who appeared very calm**, was in fact quite worried about the situation, but he planned to say it was all made up by the media.

👍 "The spaceship **that was in our backyard**," Puneet noted, "seems to have disintegrated."

👍 The United States, **which appears to have been the focal point of the invasion**, was in incredible disarray.

I discuss earlier the confusion of *that* and *which*. *That* traditionally introduces *essential* (sometimes called *restrictive*) elements and is not usually preceded by a comma. *Which* usually introduces *additional, background* information and is preceded by a comma.

That is complicated, though. Gerald Nelson has an excellent discussion of what he calls "The Four That's" (44). *That* can be more than just a relative pronoun (easily recognized in this role since *which* can replace it: "The car *that* I like"; "The car, *which* I like"). It can also be a "complementizer," a word that transforms what follows into a complement:

👍 **That** was worrisome. [*That* = worrisome.]

👎 **Which** was worrisome. [*Which* cannot be a subject.]

👍 Puneet realized **that** he was more worried than he had ever been. [*That* introduces a complement. Note that the *that* can be omitted here with no loss of meaning.]

That can also be used as an adverb that emphasizes an adjective:

👍 It wasn't **that** bad.

Keep in mind, too, that it is frequently used as a demonstrative pronoun:[4]

👍 **That** day lived more in infamy than December 7, 1941.

Indefinite Pronouns

Indefinite pronouns include *one, someone, somebody, no one, none, neither, everyone,* and *everybody*. These often take a subject position in your sentence, but it's sometimes unclear whether they take a singular or plural verb. Traditionally, these take singular verbs, but sometimes a plural verb is acceptable, especially if an intervening prepositional phrase suggests plurality. Some audiences reject the use of plural verbs with indefinite pronouns, but it seems to me that the issue is nuanced.

👍 In fact, **none** of the aliens was bellicose. [Singular.]

👍 Puneet and Arpita did some investigating of what was happening in their town, but **neither** of them was happy about the results. [Singular.]

---

[4]   See table 2, and later, pages 106–7.

👍 "**None** of the people I've talked to are willing to go on the record with their opinions," Arpita said. [Conceptually plural. Many precisians would opt for the singular *is* here, though a rephrasing that omitted the *their* would be necessary.]

👍 **Everybody's** routines were damaged. [Note that in the possessive, this pronoun takes an apostrophe + s, as does *somebody* or *anybody*.]

👎 **Everyone** she met were confused. [Should be "was" even though the *everyone* refers to a group of people. Why is this? When used in this way, *everyone* suggests or means *every single person*.]

But here is an interesting situation: if you introduce *everyone* in one clause, it will typically take a singular, but if your sentence moves to a new clause, *everyone* acquires a plural quality:

👍 **Everyone** she met **was** confused, but when Arpita talked to **them**, she was heartened to discover how resilient **they were** proving to be.

When you use an indefinite pronoun, think about it. Consider whether you want to suggest plural or singular. You need to make a conscious choice in these situations: What will augment your meaning? What will be most understandable to an audience? Indefinite pronouns are technically singular, but if your sentence suggests a strong plurality or you switch clauses (as in the preceding example), you need to switch to plural.

Demonstrative Pronouns

This group of pronouns, any of which can function as a sentence's subject, includes *this* (singular, something nearby), *that* (singular, something at a distance), *these* (plural, something nearby), and *those* (plural, something at a distance). These words seem straightforward but are sometimes confused. You need to make sure that you keep the number (singular versus plural) straight, and you also want to think about whether the item you're referring to is nearby or farther away, either literally or metaphorically.

> 👍 "**These** toenail-mons are impossible to read," Arpita sighed one morning.

> 👎 "Yeah, **these** device are hard to use without Toespex," Puneet said. But on the other hand, do you really need all **those** biometric?" [Should be "these devices" and **these biometrics.** Actually and surprisingly, I am seeing this error more and more often.]

> 👍 "Devices," Arpita said, sighing. Then she realized Puneet was joking. "I'm beginning to think that **these** things are controlling our lives."

Another common error is using the object pronoun in place of the demonstrative.

> 👎 "Get **them** aliens out of our backyards!" Garrastazu screamed. [Should be "Get these aliens out of our backyards. (Or, "Get those . . .")]

This is understandable in speech (it's regional slang), but it would be inappropriate in any setting that required formal English.

Additional Pronoun Cases

Interrogative pronouns start questions: *who, what, where, how, why, when* are in this category. *Indefinite relative pronouns* are words like *whoever, whatever, wherever,* and *whichever.*

I should note that when someone responds to a question or assertion with *whatever*, it suggests that that person does not feel the question or assertion is worthy of an answer. *Whatever* has assumed a passive-aggressive quality.

Whatever can also be used in a straightforward manner too, though, with no implicit aggressiveness:

👍 Puneet said, "On vacation, I can do **whatever** I want."

👍 His colleague Selina replied, "**Whatever**."

You should probably minimize your use of what is sometimes called an *anticipatory pronoun*—namely, a pronoun that occurs prior to the antecedent. This kind of pronoun forces the reader to suspend understanding for a little too long. In these examples, the antecedent is in italics and the pronoun in boldface:

👎 👍 **They** didn't know what to do or even whether they were lucky, *those people whose houses were not invaded.*

👎 👍 Out early in the next morning, taking shooting practice by knocking bottles off **his** fence, was *Garrastazu.*

These constructions are interesting because they vary typical word order, but they might puzzle your reader. People don't want to wait that long for an antecedent, a word that (as its name implies) usually comes before the pronoun.

Who or Whom?

The *who/whom* distinction causes no end of frustration for most people, unless the sentence's construction is quite simple and recognizable, as in "Who did that?" (no one would say

"Whom did that?" I don't believe), or in the venerable "To Whom It May Concern." When you write, you usually have time enough to go back to revise, but when you speak, you need to swiftly decide whether you want *who* or *whom*.

Fortunately, we're discussing writing here. Put your finger over the *who* or *whom* in the sentence you are working on. Then decide what's missing from the relative clause (again, this is a group of words with subject and verb and that your *who* or *whom* is modifying) near the *who(m)* that your finger is obscuring. If in that clause you can easily put a *she* or *he* or *they*, then it is missing a subject. Thus *who* is correct. If *her*, *him*, or *them* fits, then you should use *whom*. Here is an example of a sentence where you have to decide which pronoun is best:

👍 "A man [who or whom] I know has decided to go to Iceland," Puneet noted.

Put your finger on or strike through the "who or whom":

👍 "A man ~~who or whom~~ I know has decided to go to Iceland," Puneet noted.

"I know" is the relative clause including the "who/whom." Would you say "I know *he*" or "I know *him*"? Since it's *him*, the case is objective, so "whom" is the word you want. (It's only fair to add, though, that here the *whom* can be omitted with no loss of meaning.)

Here is another, slightly less reliable but a lot simpler method. If the word directly following the *who* or *whom* is a verb that is working with that pronoun, it should be *who*:

👍 "A man I know *who is* going to Iceland told me his fears weren't of aliens but of us."

In short, nouns and pronouns are parts of speech that refer to things or people, the physical or psychological essences of the world. While John Robert Ross labels nouns as "cold," as the "ultimate zero," their frozen-in-placeness has, I think, a comforting solidity. They're the rock-solid stanchions of our language, the things or persons that an audience imagines and personally animates. Thus we need to make sure that these words retain their fixed shapes, that there is no confusion as to whether they're plural or singular; male, female, or neither. Nouns are the solid parts of the verbal universe that endure, elements that remain after everything else is washed away, and as I suggest earlier, have their slightly less frigid variants, like gerunds and appositives.

Of course, the words we use to make these "cold" nouns really come to life—to warm up a lot—also have great importance. Modifying words enliven noun forms, making them distinctive and memorable. They help depict what these nouns are really like in all their specificity, what's special, unique, different, strange, striking, or remarkable about them. In a similar way, we have words that specify and narrow the meaning of verb forms; that tell when, where, and how our verbs' actions take place. Part 3 explores how to use adjectives to modify or accentuate certain features of nouns, and how to use adverbs to temper, specify, and detail the manner in which verbs and adjectives convey meaning.

PART THREE
Complexity

Early in her final novel *A Breath of Life*, Brazilian writer Clarice Lispector makes an enigmatic and insightful remark: "Life has no adjective." I think she means that there is no single word that captures life's constant flow of novelty. She goes on to say, "It's a mixture in a strange crucible" (10), her only adjective being *strange*.

Still, we can make an effort to describe that "strange crucible" or some aspects of it. That's what this part is about: capturing the complexity of life—or at least of what you're writing about. How do you find words to express the contradictory-and-convoluted-essence-of, the impossible-to-find-an-adjective-for thing, event, or person that you want to delineate with accuracy, verve, and originality?

No one promised you that writing would be easy.

While nouns and verbs form the core, the pith, the still and solid lub-dubby heart of your communication, the many small modifying words surrounding your nouns and verbs serve to focus, narrow down, and delineate more strikingly exactly what you mean. You need to deftly employ these small words to help provide the flavor and color, the contour and texture, the warp and woof of what you want to get across. These words do a great deal to help you capture your exact meaning.

5

Modifiers

ADJECTIVES

Adjectives clearly inspire writers. Anne Carson, one of today's finest poets, writes, "Adjectives seem fairly innocent additions but look again. These small, imported mechanisms are in charge of attaching everything in the world to its place in particularity. They are the latches of being" (4). These words, in addition to adverbs, prepositions, conjunctions, and articles, form the basis of this part; they will serve as its latches of being.

> **Adjectives** modify nouns. "**Modify**" here means that they specify something about a noun; they assign to it a particular meaning that elaborates, details, colors, or narrows down the meaning of its unmodified form. Adjectives are single words, but an entire phrase or clause can function adjectivally.

To echo Anne Carson's idea, these words convey particular elements of meaning. What, for example, is the difference between a *distinct* possibility and a *distant* possibility? Between a *careful* surgery and a *careless* one? It's the difference between two universes. But still, as the poet Rae Armantrout writes,

"Terrific"
and "terrible"
are cousins after all. (68–69)

Many adjectives that sound alike have opposite meanings but retain a certain obscure linkage. There is a certain logic to this.

Forms of Adjectives

The three forms of adjectives include the base form, the comparative form, and the superlative form: *scary, scarier, scariest*. These three forms of adjective usually follow the same pattern: *nice, nicer, nicest*; *strong, stronger, strongest*; *weird, weirder, weirdest*. Some are irregular, such as *good, better, best*; *bad, worse, worst*; *much, more, most*. (Note that *badder* and *baddest* have found their way into slang, though it's best to avoid them in formal writing.) When you use a superlative form, it is almost always preceded by *the*: *the worst, the best, the most considerate*.

When you want to create a comparative or superlative form for some adjectives, they take a *more* and a *most*. For example, *intelligent* does not have a comparative or superlative form (*intelligenter* or *intelligentest*). You need instead to say *more intelligent* or *most intelligent*. Long adjectives like *beautiful, luxurious, terrible, palpable, vituperative* also do not have comparative or superlative forms. Some, like *vivid*, which can take the forms *vivider* or *vividest*, are problematic: these two forms are in *The American Heritage Dictionary* but do not appear in most other dictionaries. (Dictionaries often disagree about matters of this sort.) It's euphony rather than simply word length that seems to be the decisive factor. If the *-er* and *-est* suffixes (endings) sound odd or are difficult to pronounce, then it's probably a good idea to use *more* or *most*: *more vivid, most vivid.*

I should add too that using *most* or *more* is possible with any adjective, even ones with a comparative or superlative form: *most worthy, most strong, more naughty.* Using *most* or *more* slightly changes the meaning of the expression, making it more formal, possibly even ceremonial:

👍 Puneet wrote, "The world's leaders are *more* weak and helpless than anyone imagined; individual citizens, though, are proving *more* stout, *more* fierce, and *more* brave than they have ever been."

Variations in Meaning of Adjectives

Not too surprisingly, the meaning of the adjective you use directly depends on the surrounding context. For example, here are some sentences in which the same adjectives take on quite different meanings:

👍 When the aliens emerged from their vessels, many people feared they might be *wicked.*

👎 👍 "Did you see them slither along the ground?" Puneet exclaimed to his wife. "They are *wicked fast.*" [Note that "wicked" used this way is a New England regionalism, not acceptable in formal written English.]

👍 The smell of the alien spaceships was overpoweringly *strong.*

👍 Puneet developed an exercise program to make him fit and *strong.*

👍 It appeared that after the aliens left their ships, the exits were locked *fast*.

👍 Congress was *fast* to condemn the president for this invasion.

👎 Meanwhile, *fast*-food restaurants continued to be overrun with customers.

The adjectives' meanings are critical in differentiating the meanings of these example sentences. You can see why Carson calls adjectives the "latches of being."

Verb Forms Used Adjectivally

As I mentioned earlier, verb forms can function as adjectives. Many words that end in *-ed* or *-ing*, derived from verbs, fall into this category. These words, called *participles* (see pp. 34–37), modify nouns or pronouns and can come prior to or after the noun being modified:

👎 *Wanting* to be helpful, Puneet knocked on his neighbor's door.

👍 People were inside, but Puneet's knock went *unanswered*. His presence was not *wanted* there. He could see through the window that no one was *enMeshed*. Odd.

👎 Arpita, for her part, remained *focused* on her work.

👎 The article she was writing would be appear in tomorrow's paper. Her *published* writing was always impressive.

👎 *Longing* for clarity, Arpita tried to make sure that her prose reached a large audience.

👍 She was very *talented*. [Note that this adjective takes the same form as the others but does not derive from a verb but from the noun "talent." It's not in fact a participle. Writing in the early nineteenth century, the great English writer Samuel Taylor Coleridge denounced it as "barbarous," which seems to me a bit strong.[1] Other words, like *ivied* or *venomed*, take the same form, as there is no verb *to ivy* or *to venom*.]

Relative Clauses

In addition to single-word adjectives, *relative clauses*, as mentioned earlier in the section on relative pronouns, are groups of words usually introduced by *who*, *whose*, *which*, or *that*, and they function adjectivally:

👍 Puneet and Arpita realized the house *that they loved* was now being used as a home for slimy, shimmering, alien puddle entities. [*That* may be omitted here with no loss of meaning.]

👍 Their living room, *which had been so carefully furnished and arranged*, was a favorite spot for the invaders.

---

[1]   Here is how Coleridge puts it: "I regret to see that vile and barbarous vocable *talented*, stealing out of the newspapers into the leading reviews and most respectable publications of the day. Why not *shillinged*, *farthinged*, *tenpenced*, &c.? The formation of a participle passive from a noun is a licence that nothing but a very peculiar felicity can excuse. If mere convenience is to justify such attempts upon the idiom, you cannot stop till the language becomes, in the proper sense of the word, corrupt. Most of these pieces of slang come from America" (8 July 1832). One shudders to think what Coleridge would make of social media, the Internet, or chatbots.

That is sometimes used—incorrectly—in reference to people. It seems to me more deserving of Coleridge's epithet "barbarous":

   👎 A man **that** he knew since graduate school had taken steps to stop the invasion. [Should be *whom he knew*—or omit the relative pronoun altogether.]

We often reduce sentences down, omitting certain elements that might be silently understood. Thus, by omitting a noun that's taken as obvious, you can turn adjectives into nouns:

   👍 The *Eurasians* [shortened version of *Eurasian leaders and media*] report that there are no aliens invading their country.

   👍 The *poor* [shortened version of *poor people*] suffer the most of all during the crisis.

   👍 👎 The *old captain* the ship of state—the usual situation in most countries nowadays. [*Old* is a shortened version of *old people*.]

These shortened forms, called *nominal adjectives*, can sometimes be confusing, as in the third sentence, which is grammatical but still in need of revision. You want to make sure that your reader knows when your adjective is functioning as a noun and when as just a modifier. Here it initially looks as though the subject of the sentence is the noun phrase *The old captain*, but in fact the subject is the nominal adjective *old*. The verb is captain. (The sentence is an example of a "garden-path" sentence, one that's grammatically correct but communicatively misleading. Hence I give it the "thumbs-up/thumbs-down" sign.)

Prepositions and Placement of Modifiers in Sentences

Prepositional phrases can function as adjectives, modifying either another adjective or a noun. (Prepositions also can work as adverbs.) The italicized portions in the following sentences are prepositional phrases that function as adjectives:

- 👍 Puneet and Arpita's lives became impossibly busy since the landing *of the aliens*.

- 👍 Everyone's life was different; no one could ignore this massive change *in the population of earth*.

- 👍 Some people reacted with fear, some with disgust, while many just tried to accept the presence *of these weird puddle people*.

- 👎 "Someone is *at the door with a package*," Arpita called to her husband.

- 👍 "Our door has a package?" Puneet responded, somewhat facetiously.

Why do I give the "thumbs-down" emoji to the one sentence? (And why does Puneet make fun of it?) The situation is actually a familiar one: we have two prepositional phrases side by side. The first, *at the door*, is adverbial (it modifies "is," answering the implied question, "Where?"); and the second one, *with a package*, is adjectival, modifying *someone*. Puneet's reply to his wife indicates that her placing the adjectival phrase right after *door* opens up the possibility that that phrase is modifying *door*, even though that seems a little absurd. Here is a revision:

- 👍 "What I meant was that someone with a package is at the door," Arpita said.

This slight reordering puts *with a package* directly after what it's modifying—that is, *someone*. It also places the (adverbial) prepositional phrase *at the door,* which modifies *is,* directly after that verb.

Your placement of modifiers is important. It has to be clear to your reader which noun (or in the case of an adverb, which verb, other adverb, or adjective) you are modifying. And sometimes, the misplacement of a modifier generates strange sentences, ones that evoke an "absurd universe," where doors might have packages, say.

Here are a few sentences that exhibit problems with the use of adjectives:

- 🖒 With the alien crisis to report on and with a wife to support, Puneet's computer was always at the ready. [Does the computer have a wife? After the comma, the next clause needs to start with *Puneet.*]

- 🖒 Exhausted by all his reporting and writing, the alien invasion proved how valuable Puneet was. [Was the alien invasion reporting? After the comma, the next clause needs to start with *Puneet.*]

- 🖒 "I have a terrible writer's block," Puneet said, but then quickly revised. "I mean I have a terrible *case* of writer's block!" [He revises because an adjective can modify more than one noun in a given sentence. In his first version, *terrible* can modify either *writer* or *writer's block.*]

- 🖒 The Eurasian president spoke to the Western media, testy as always. [The sentence needs to make clearer who is *testy as always,* the Eurasian president or the media. I would open the sentence using that phrase.]

In general, it's best to keep adjectives close to the word they modify, usually prior to the noun, but sometimes after it:

👍 Something *frightening* was happening to earth. It was as *unprecedented* as the ten-year plague earlier in the century.

👍 The politicians *in charge* didn't really know what to do.

👍 The aliens, *quiet and nonthreatening,* were not communicating in any way.

Sequencing of Adjectives

Long adjective strings are unusual in formal writing. From time to time in fiction you will find long lists of adjectives, and this is allowable, sometimes even effective. But in general (and this is a stylistic suggestion), you want to keep in mind what's sometimes called "the power of threes": limit your adjectives to three at the very most when you are writing formal English. But it is finally your choice, not a rule.

The Grammar Book by Diane Larsen-Freeman and Marianne Celce-Murcia presents the sequence of adjective use in English, a sequence that is based on how people actually use English:

opinion|size|shape|condition|age|color|origin (394)

Grant Barrett, a linguist and dictionary editor, offers a slightly different sequence:

number|quality/value|size|temperature|shape|color| origin|material (159)

In the most recent revision (third edition) of Larsen-Freeman and Celce-Murcia's book, however, the authors omit the chart, perhaps recognizing that the sequence is more fluid and idiosyncratic than they had previously thought.

In fact, any prescription of sequence is likely to be debatable and frequently violated by native speakers. In general you want to move from "opinion" (or "quality/value"), to "size," "shape" (which could include "age" or "condition"), to "color" and "origin." Here is an example with five adjectives in a row:

> 👍 The aliens were *strange, puddle-sized, amorphous, translucent,* and *otherworldly.*

This is acceptable for describing a physical object, but often adjectives describe feelings, ideas, or other abstractions:

> 👍 Many theories were advanced about the invaders, theories that were *uninformed, self-contradictory, tendentious, inflammatory,* and sometimes *paranoid.*

All of these adjectives reflect opinions. Why did I pick this order, though? I start with what seems to me more or less objectively provable and readily accepted ("uninformed" and "self-contradictory"), and then move to two adjectives that offer stronger value judgments ("tendentious" is a value judgment about the lack of objectivity of the theories, and "inflammatory" is a value judgment about the motives of those putting forth the theories). I end with a controversial, conclusive value judgment: "paranoid." The last three adjectives increase their condemnation of the theories, and using the rhetorical device of "climax," position the most extreme value judgment as the concluding one.

Here is another example, one in which I move from more or less obvious objective description, through some mild value judgments, to a climactic zinger:

👍 In deciding how the United States might respond to the invasion, Congress was *strident, polarized, bewildered, savage,* and *spineless.*

One thing you want to keep in mind when generating these lists is that the adjectives must be mutually exclusive—no synonyms are allowed. And the longer the list, the more difficult this becomes.

"Latches of Being" Revisited

Adjectives do indeed function very significantly in communicating the complexity of our ideas; their "latches of being" quality becomes less hyperbolic the more closely one looks. Huddleston and Pullum offer a gracefully understated but powerful expression of the importance of this part of speech:

If a language has adjectives, it will always have one that means "good" (an adjective denoting the property of having positive worth or value), and nearly always another meaning "bad"; virtually always it will have a size adjective meaning "large"; and probably also one meaning "small," and some others; it is extremely likely to have an adjective meaning "old," may well have another meaning "young" or "new," and it is very likely to have some color adjectives meaning "black," "white," "red," "green," etc. The core semantic function of adjectives seems to be to provide terms for individual properties of the kinds just listed, and usually other properties as well: physical properties like hardness and heaviness, human tendencies like kindness and cruelty, properties like speed of movement, and so on. (527–28)

Good or bad; big or small; young or old; black, white, or in color; hard or soft; heavy or light; kind or cruel; fast or slow— these aspects of our *Umwelt* or personal environment are vitally important to humans across all cultures, and languages reflect that importance, as they refract the complexity of life itself. Life may have no adjective, but adjectives themselves have a kind of life.

6

Modifiers

ADVERBS

This part of speech modifies verbs, adjectives, and other adverbs. Adverbs can even modify an entire sentence. They tend to answer questions such as the following:

"When?" (adverbs like *now, until, again, soon, sometimes*);

"In what way?" (adverbs like *happily, fondly, pleasantly, tiredly, crazily, swiftly*);

"Where?" (adverbs that give direction, position, or distance, like *upward, downward, inside of, outside of*);

"How?" (adverbs like *arguably, honestly, personally, frankly, confidentially, possibly, probably, likely, certainly, maybe*);

"Why?" (adverbs like *in case, so that, in order to, because, since*);

"To what extent?" (adverbs like *very, somewhat, extremely*).

Kolln, Gray, and Salvatore point out that we can derive adverbs from adjectives:

The -ly means "like": quickly = quick-like; happily = happy-like. . . .

In addition to these "adverbs of manner," as the -ly adverbs are called, we have a selection of other adverbs that undergo no changes of form, among them *then, now, here, there, everywhere, afterward, often, sometimes, seldom, always.* (23)

It's good to keep in mind that many words can function as either an adjective or an adverb:

👍 These were the *best* years of his life, Puneet realized. [Adjective.]

👍 He exercised *best* on an empty stomach. [Adverb.]

👍 Arpita was certainly the *best*-prepared writer on the staff. [Adverb.]

Well, which is always adverbial when used as a modifier, can be substituted for *best* in the last two sentences here (though their meaning alters), which indicates that *best* is adverbial.

Adverbs take a wide variety of forms. Many but not all end in -*ly*. Some words that are not adverbs end in -*ly* as well. (*Folly*, for example, is a noun; *rally* is a noun or verb.) They may be positioned in various locations in a sentence, not needing to be so tightly tied as adjectives must be to that which they modify.

Despite their relative mobility, though, adverbs can cause some of the same problems as adjectives. You as a writer need to structure your sentence so it's clear which word your adverb is modifying. Many prepositional phrases can function as both adjectives and adverbs, too, so your sentence structure has to make very clear which word is being modified by your adverb or adverbial phrase.

Adverb Placement

Let's start by looking at placement of adverbs. This can be right next to a verb or separated by a few words:

- 👍 Many people urged the president to *immediately* declare war on the invaders.

- 👍 Many people urged the president to declare war *immediately* on the invaders.

- 👍 Many people urged the president *immediately* to declare war on the invaders.

All of these are fine, even though the first splits the infinitive, *to declare.* But again, as I note earlier, that's OK. If someone objects, give them a Bronx cheer. Here are some problem placements, though:

- 👎 "Figuring out how to respond and deal with these aliens *effectively* is our top priority," the president declared. [I would place *effectively* in between *to* and *respond*; otherwise, it's not clear if it modifies the words before it or after it. As it stands, the sentence contains what's called a "squinting modifier": it looks both ways, modifying either "how to respond and deal with" or "our top priority."]

- 👎 It was an issue of mostly national security. [Place *mostly* directly after the verb *was* or at the start of the sentence.]

- 👎 Puneet and Arpita were not involved in any high-level negotiations about the situation *personally*. [Not clear enough what the *personally* modifies; it "dangles" at the end.]

The use of *only* is slightly problematic since the word can modify so many different things and can make sense almost anywhere:

- 👍 They were *only* concerned with figuring out what was going on.

- 👍 They were concerned with *only* figuring out what was going on.

- 👍 *Only* they were concerned with figuring out what was going on.

- 👍 They *only* were concerned with figuring out what was going on.

Note how these four sentences all have slightly different emphases. Only the third sentence has a significantly different meaning. All of these are correct, but you need to decide what exactly you want to get across. They all make sense, but what is the sense that you want to convey?

Larsen-Freeman and Celce-Murcia report that about 75 percent of adverbials are actually prepositional phrases, citing D. O. Miller's oft-referred-to but unpublished master's thesis. Here are some situations in which a prepositional phrase functions adverbially:

- 👍 Because no unified response emerged from the government, many people decided to respond, and *with their personal weapons*, they attacked the invaders.

- 👎 People fought daily *with their guns, pipe bombs, and homemade grenades.* [It sounds as though they are fighting against their own weaponry, so the sentence needs rephrasing.]

👍 These weapons, wielded *by a surprising number* of gun owners, ruined much property and injured scores of people. [*Of gun owners* and *of people* are adjectivally used.]

👍 But many citizens, who acted *without much hope for success*, just allowed the alien puddle people to reside *in the comfort of their homes*. [Note that *of their homes* is adjectival, modifying *comfort*.]

Sometimes the prepositional phrase can be replaced with a single adverb (in the last example, *comfortably* could substitute for *in the comfort of*, though the *of* would have to be replaced with *in*), but sometimes the whole phrase is necessary.

Forms of Adverbs

Like adjectives, adverbs have comparative and superlative forms. Some are one-word variants, like *badly, worse, worst*; or *well, better, best*. With most adverbs, if you want to increase the intensity of one of the comparatives, you can use *much, most*, or *very* before it: *much stronger, much milder, much better, very softly, most pleasantly*.

👍 The situation was *much worse* and at the same time *much better* than anyone had imagined.

Adverbs can often indicate degrees of intensity of a verb or adjective that they modify. Here are some, ordered from greatest to least intensity:

utterly, totally, entirely, incredibly, excessively, exceptionally, absolutely, remarkably, really, remarkably, very, fairly, pretty, somewhat, rather, slightly, mildly, understatedly, a little

Adverbs can be classified as "boosters" or "downtoners" (Nelson 68). Boosters are all the preceding words up to and including *very*; after that, the rest are downtoners. Here are some intensity adverbs in sentences:

👍 While a significant segment of the population was *incredibly* alarmed and aggressive, most people were *fairly* sure that the aliens were not dangerous.

👍 Still, everyone was *extremely* curious about what would happen next, and they spent even more time than usual enMeshed, searching for answers to their questions.

Note that these adverbs all modify adjectives.

Conjunctive Adverbs

Conjunctive adverbs often cause problems for writers. These include words like *however, consequently, therefore, thus, furthermore, nevertheless, for example*, and *meanwhile*. They typically perform some work of connecting main clauses in a sentence, but (as I mentioned in part 1) lack the joining capacity of the ABSOFNY words (*and, but, so, or, for, nor, yet*). You may use a conjunctive adverb in the middle of a sentence; however, it needs to have a semicolon before it (as this very sentence has). A semicolon can also appear after a conjunctive adverb, however; the deciding factor is what you are wanting to get across.

Here are some other examples of conjunctive adverb use, with the conjunctive adverb in italics:

Adding information:

👍 The problem was that people were confused; *moreover*, many were armed.

👍 The nail-mons gave extensive biometric data; *for example*, they could be tapped through to provide blood pressure, pulse, EKG normalcy, blood sugar levels, a lipid profile, and about a hundred additional pieces of data.

Offering a comparison:

👍 The invasion rankled millions; *similarly*, people started resenting and distrusting the media.

Presenting a contrast:

👍 Puneet and Arpita worked to gather information; *on the other hand*, the situation was changing so rapidly that it was often unclear what was going on.

Suggesting a result or a cause and effect:

👍 Weaponry had no effect on the aliens; *hence*, people just began to accept the invaders.

Giving emphasis:

👍 The aliens were totally otherworldly; *indeed*, they seemed to be from another dimension.

Indicating a time period:

👍 The first few weeks witnessed a widespread panic; *subsequently*, though, it diminished.

Placing conditions on something:

👍 People were asked to surrender their arms to the police; *otherwise*, they would go to prison.

The following sentences exemplify common problems with the use of conjunctive adverbs:

👎 It seemed as though all the spaceships had landed *however* people were still worried that the invasion would ramp up. [This is a fused sentence. The easiest way to revise would be to place a semicolon after *landed*, and a comma after *however.*]

👎 The people who had not been afraid of the aliens got used to them, *indeed*, many considered them equivalent to pets that never ate and never had to be walked. [This is a comma splice. I'd place a semicolon, not a comma, after *them.*]

👎 Still, though, people described the alien experience in wildly differing ways, *for example*, some people saw them as friendly and benign, while others saw them as sinister. [Another comma splice. A semicolon, not a comma, is needed after *ways*. Alternatively, forming two separate sentences also works.]

However, which is often used as a conjunctive adverb, presents further difficulties since it also can be used as an "interruptive" or as a "concessive." An "interruptive" is a word that indicates a pause in the middle of a thought. Most of the conjunctive adverbs can be used in this manner:

👍 People wanted, *however*, to achieve some sort of stable condition.

👍 Puneet and Arpita's reporting, *meanwhile*, had been widely syndicated, and it suggested that such stability was far off.

A "concessive" is a word that sort of concedes something; in the case of *however*, it means *in whatever manner or no matter how*:

👍 Puneet and Arpita knew that *however* hard they tried, their efforts at getting the truth out would not be enough to sway much of the populace.

👍 What was the truth, though? *However* strange these aliens were, it seemed, they had no intention of colonizing earth and were neither aggressive nor harmful. Still, they were a strange new addition to everyone's lives.

Well versus *Good*

When do you use *well* and when *good*? *Well* modifies verbs, adjectives, or adverbs; *good* modifies nouns. Yet *well* seems to be falling out of favor. For example, one of my colleagues advertised her car for sale in a local newspaper in rural Washington. She had written, "Runs well." *Well* modifies how the car runs. "It runs well" is correct. But such a phrasing did not succeed: she got no response to her ad. The next week, she changed the phrasing to "Runs good," and ten calls came in the next day.

I asked my students about this, and they said that "runs good" simply sounds more persuasive than "runs well." "Runs well," they told me, summons up "runs, well, sort of"; by contrast, "runs good" means "a good runner, a good machine." I was skeptical.

How about "I feel well" as opposed to "I feel good"? This is a situation where we have a "health adjective" (*well*), which should be used when discussing matters of health, as in "I feel well." A similar one is "I feel faint." In these cases, even though *well* and *faint* are typically adverbs, here they are acting as adjectives.

To say "I feel good" suggests that a person feels, senses, somehow experiences positiveness:

👍 Puneet felt good about his prospects for promotion at the newspaper.

However, using *good* ("Do you feel good?") in reference to one's health or psychological state is quite common in speech. Like the car that "runs good," it will continue on, I expect, for some time.

PART FOUR
Confidence

While your writing should make your reader confident in your credibility and authority, it should also display a sense of confidence, of certainty and naturalness, even when you are trying to express difficult, complex ideas. One aspect of sentence construction that might help increase an audience's confidence in your writing is how effortlessly and accurately you use determiners.[1] If you did not grow up speaking English, sometimes you might choose a determiner that sounds foreign or strange to native speakers. There are often options as to which determiner can be used in a sentence, one determiner meaning one thing, and another meaning quite something else. You need to choose the determiner that supports the meaning you are trying to get across.

Chapter 7 defines the three major classes of determiners (predeterminers, central determiners, and postdeterminers)

---

[1]   This section on determiners benefited enormously from comments by my colleague Gerard M. Dalgish, Emeritus Professor of English at the City University of New York. In this chapter I will frequently quote his comments from personal correspondence with me.

and attempts to conceptualize their use. Chapter 8 focuses largely on the various uses of *the* (the definite article) and offers a series of concrete suggestions about how to decide when to use *the*, *a/an*, or no article at all, which is labeled as ∅ or the "zero article."

Determiners are words that can be many different parts of speech—adjectives, articles, pronouns—and they establish the limits of what a noun might mean. They indicate whether the person, place, or thing belongs to someone; whether it's one of a kind; whether it's a special or maybe famous thing; whether it's near or far; plural or singular. Thus the determiner you choose is an integral part of your meaning.

Determiners include words that indicate possession: *my*, *your*, *his*, *our*. They also include *this*, *that*, *those*, *these*, *all*, *both*, *many*, *much*, or similar words that give important information about a noun, including its location and whether it's plural or singular. In addition, they mark whether the noun following them is something specific (definite article *the*) or something general (indefinite articles *a* or *an*).

7

Predeterminers, Central Determiners, and Postdeterminers

Predeterminers

These words come before a noun, early in the sentence. They include *quantifiers*—words suggesting a number—such as *one of, each, every, any, all, a few, a number of, none of, both, twice, double*. *Of* is optional with most predeterminers, though with *none*, the *of*-phrase is required:

- 👍 *None of* the aliens communicated with people. [We would never write or say, *None the aliens.*]

- 👍 *Each of* the country's households, it soon emerged, housed at least one alien.

- 👍 *Each* individual seemed to have a different response to the invaders.

- 👍 *A few* aliens seemed reluctant to leave their vessels. [*A few of the* would also work.]

Contrast this last sentence, though, with the following, which has a very different meaning:

- 👍 *Few* aliens seemed reluctant to leave their vessels.

A few means "there are a small but a possibly significant number." *Few* means "there are almost none, but some."

Another predeterminer category is *intensifiers*, including words like *rather, quite, such, what*. These must be paired with an *a* or an *an*, as follows:

   👍 *Such a* situation was alarming to everyone.

   👍 *What a* shame that no one could communicate with these things!

   👍 *Quite a few* people took leave of their senses, sad to say.

Multipliers (*three times a day*) and *fractions* (*two-thirds* of the populace) can also function as predeterminers.

   👍 *Ten times a day*, warning sirens would go off, but most people stopped worrying about those, stopped even hearing them.

Central Determiners

This group includes articles (*a/an, the*), which cause the majority of determiner difficulties for nonnative speakers of English. Native speakers do not typically have much trouble with these, yet (unless they are linguists) they can rarely explain why they use one determiner rather than another.

Usually the indefinite article, *a/an*, appears prior to a noun that is unfamiliar, generalized, generic, or nonspecific; the definite article *the*, by contrast, comes before a noun that is specific, particular, and familiar to both speaker and listener.

Central determiners also include possessive forms (*my, his, her, our, their*), and demonstrative pronouns like *these, those, that, this*.

Figure 1 gives an overview of how to use the central determiners that are the most difficult, *a/an*, *the*, or no determiner at all, sometimes referred to as ∅. You might want to bookmark this flowchart while you read through this chapter and the next, as you'll probably want to refer back to it multiple times in order to help you visualize the process of choosing the right determiner.

Central determiners are not typically combined, I should point out. You need to pick the single one that fits best within your sentence. The following are sentences that most people would never think of generating:

 ☙ *This the* situation was unprecedented.

 ☙ *His that* strategy was simple: gather as much information as possible.

 ☙ *Our this* the country was in peril.

Proper Nouns (Names)

Proper nouns are names (of people, of cities or countries, or of geographical formations such as rivers, mountains, statues, or monuments).

When deciding which central determiner to use prior to a proper noun, you need to determine first off whether the noun is singular or plural, and second, if it is representative of a class or category of things. These are the two key factors in choosing the right central determiner to use.

Singular Proper Nouns

These nouns, the names of people, place names, manufacturers, brands, or the like, usually do not take a determiner:

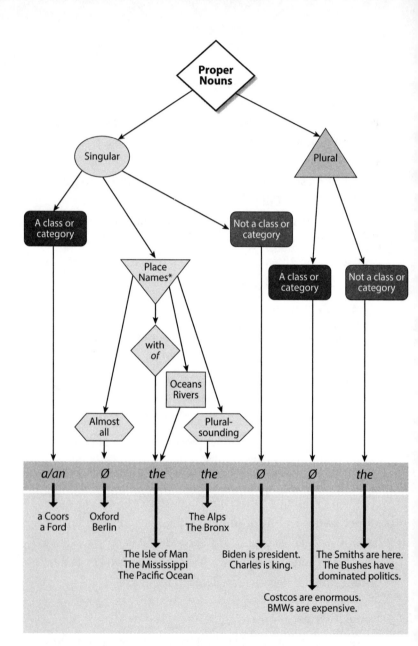

FIGURE 1. The process of choosing between *the*, *a*, and no article (∅) before a noun.

* There are some exceptions to these rules, such as *Queens* (no article) or *the Antarctic*. See chapter 8.

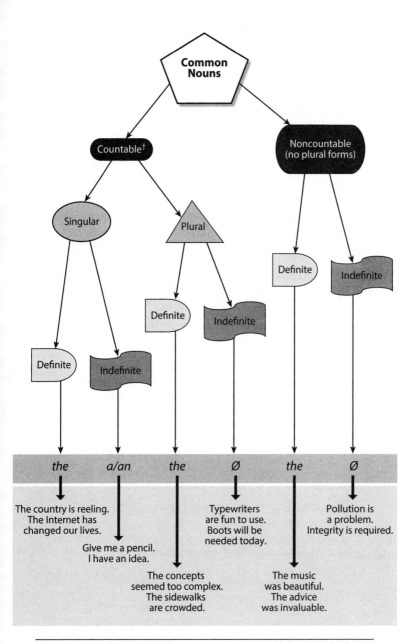

Common Nouns

Countable†
- Singular
  - Definite → *the*
    - The country is reeling.
    - The Internet has changed our lives.
  - Indefinite → *a/an*
    - Give me a pencil.
    - I have an idea.
- Plural
  - Definite → *the*
    - The concepts seemed too complex.
    - The sidewalks are crowded.
  - Indefinite → Ø
    - Typewriters are fun to use.
    - Boots will be needed today.

Noncountable (no plural forms)
- Definite → *the*
  - The music was beautiful.
  - The advice was invaluable.
- Indefinite → Ø
  - Pollution is a problem.
  - Integrity is required.

---

† Some nouns can be either countable or noncountable and follow the rules for their function within the sentence.

👍 Pequa, like many towns and cities, was reeling.

👍 Puneet was very tired.

👍 Selina Guttierez, Puneet's friend from high school, always admired his work.

👍 Another woman named Selina, Selina Paz, worked at the Pequa newspaper employing Puneet and Arpita.

Sometimes it's necessary to use a central determiner (a possessive pronoun) in front of a name if you are trying to distinguish it from a different person with the same name. For example, if Arpita is talking about the reporter named Selina, she might say something like this:

👍 "Our Selina is more ambitious than your old friend Selina Guttierez."

This is, however, somewhat informal. It does also occur sometimes, usually in British English, when someone is referring to a member of their family, whom they might call "our Mary" or "our Xinyi."

If there is an "of" phrase in the proper noun, a determiner, usually *the* is needed:

👍 The old Gene Chandler song was often one that Puneet heard in his head. It went, "I'm *the* Duke *of* Earl."

👍 A few years ago, the newspaper had sent someone to *the* Statue *of* Liberty to see if it still commanded awe and respect.

Singular Proper Nouns Representing a Class or Category

Sometimes a proper noun will represent a category. In this case, you should use *a/an* before it:

👍 "**An Android** is the cell I always used to depend on," Puneet declared one day.

👍 "Right," said Arpita, "but **a Coors** seems to be what you still depend on at day's end."

Plural Proper Nouns

This variety of proper noun almost always takes the definite article, *the*:

👍 **The** Tagores were happy with each other, but they felt unnerved by the invasion.

👍 Their next-door neighbors, **the** Garrastazus, were putting Arpita and Puneet under a lot of pressure.

Plural Proper Nouns Representing a Class or Category

When representing a class or category, plural proper nouns take no article, sometimes called the zero article ($\varnothing$):

👍 Andromedas have won almost every car award imaginable.

👍 Andromedas, like most electric cars, are costly to repair.

Common Nouns

Common nouns are persons, places, or things. When deciding which determiner to use with a common noun, you need to keep three considerations in mind. First, is the noun "countable" or "noncountable"? That is your first decision point. The second decision point concerns number: is the noun singular or plural? And third, is it "definite" or "indefinite"? That is, does it refer to some particular, definite thing that the speaker and listener both know about, or by contrast (in a sense similar to the situation with proper nouns that refer to a class or category), does the noun refer to something indefinite, or more generalized and nonspecific?[1]

The initial decision you have to make is the one between countable and noncountable.

Countable nouns are things (or ideas, concepts, entities) that one can count, one by one, and have a singular and plural form: *one pen, two pens; one computer, two computers; one watch, two watches.* They usually occupy a point or volume in space or time, and they retain their shape in a more or less stable manner. A *pen* or a *wristwatch* occupies a physical space, has a definite shape, and has clear, definable boundaries.

Even forms and behaviors, which are more abstract and do not have a locale in space, can be countable nouns when they have a plural form possible, as in *habit(s), intuition(s), mood(s),* perhaps because there is something limited about them—you can look at individual examples of them—that allows for pluralization. Noncountable nouns include words like *wisdom, weather, warmth,* or *dirt.* These do not have clear, definite boundaries. Examples of some other noncountable nouns are *music, money, milk, bravery, butter, mail, rust, work, knowledge.*

Some nouns can be either countable or noncountable, depending on context: *cheese, wine, coffee.*

---

[1]   In the following chapter, I will discuss varieties of "definiteness."

Countable, Singular, Definite Nouns

If you have a singular, definite, countable noun, you usually need *the* before it, which emphasizes the fact that your audience is somewhat familiar with the noun you're discussing or that that noun is in some way being singled out as important or significant.

   ☞ Television was on, news blaring. [Should be *The* television since your audience is probably familiar with televisions.]

However, there are some situations when the determiner before a singular countable noun is elided or implied:

   👍 Print copy of the newspaper under his arm, Puneet went to work interviewing people. [*A* or *the* or *his* is implied prior to the sentence and would be OK here too.]

But in general, there is a central determiner prior to a definite, singular, countable noun:

   👍 *Our* world was gripped by nervousness. [*World* is singular, countable, and definite; *nervousness* is noncountable.]

   👍 It used to be that *the* routine people followed was repeated every day. [*Routine* is countable; definite and unique for each person.]

   👍 First, they checked to see if there was *an* invader; then, they assessed where *the* shimmering puddle had moved to overnight. [*Invader* and *shimmering puddle* are singular and countable, but the first is indefinite

(that is, some invader, not sure which one), so takes
an. The second, because it refers back to the first
noun, is thus definite and takes *the*.]

To elaborate some more, using *an* before *invader* makes sense
because it's not certain an invader will be present, and little is
known about that invader to distinguish it from any other invader. It's just *an invader,* some invader. But you want to use
the prior to *shimmering puddle* because the audience knows
that the shimmering puddles are all over—a known-about
feature of this invented world.

Some countable nouns almost always require *the*, as in
"I was in *the* hospital," the hospital being understood as a definite place we all know about—maybe the assumption being
that if you've been in one hospital, you've been in them all.[2]

Countable, Singular, Indefinite Nouns

Whenever a new situation arises, and whenever the nouns can
be assumed to be unknown or unfamiliar to the listener, indefinite articles (*a/an*) are used before them. Often *a/an* has
the effect of suggesting that the noun referred to is something
about which nothing is yet (or never will be) really known:

👍 *A* strategy for dealing with *the* alien invasion had to
be devised, despite *the* president's initial claim that *the*
invasion was all hokum. [*Strategy* is indefinite because
no particular strategy has been devised or is being
alluded to; hence *a* is needed. *The* appears before *alien*

---

2   Note that in British English this is a ∅ situation. No article is used: "I was in
hospital." Perhaps the parallel is sentences like, "I was in traction"; "I was in
school"; "I was in love." The nouns in these sentences all refer to a state of
being—and are thus classified as indefinite and noncountable.

invasion and *invasion* because this alien invasion is known about. If you put an *an* there, it would sound as though the sentence were stating some policy about alien invasions in general, which it's not. *The* before *president's initial claim* indicates also that the audience knows we are talking about Akbaliatuk and his specific, definite claim.]

👎 A hokum was not what people wanted. [This doesn't work since *hokum* is not countable. No article needed here.]

👍 An idea that some citizens embraced was mass emigration. [*Idea* is countable. Using *an* here suggests it is indefinite, one of many possible ideas. If *the* were used, it would sound as though this was the only idea that "some citizens embraced."]

👍 Puneet discovered that it was best for him to carry around *a pencil* and *a pad*; taking notes with those seemed old-fashioned but was effective. [These are indefinite—any old pencil and pad, nothing special about them.]

👎 Alien was in Puneet and Arpita's house. [Should be *An alien, One alien,* or *The alien.*]

Sometimes, prior to singular countable nouns, an *a/an* can imply *an instance* or *example of*:

👍 Like the writing of other reporters, Puneet's and Arpita's reportage was *a* determined attempt to understand truly alien consciousness.

👍 A declaration of peace and goodwill, today's editorial by Puneet and Arpita sought to assuage fear.

Countable, Plural, Definite Nouns

When you want to mention a specific group or amalgamation, *the* is used. In addition, common plural nouns that refer to definite things take a *the*:

👍 *The* alien contingent made no attempt to communicate.

👍 *The* citizens of Puneet and Arpita's town were dazed and confused. [Or, "The citizenry of the town was dazed and confused."].

Countable, Plural, Indefinite Nouns

If you are being nonspecific and discussing plural forms of a general class or type, though, the ∅ (no article) is used:

👍 Humans and animals alike suffered in varying degrees. [Note how strange this would sound if you started the sentence with a *The*. It would leave your reader wondering "which humans and animals?"]

👍 Living creatures of all kinds in fact felt threatened. Animals did not know what to make of the puddles. Plants seemed to turn away from aliens residing indoors.

When you have a plural countable noun, determiner use is often optional. But make sure that if you include a *the* with a plural noun, it's clear what exactly you are referring to—that is, make sure it's definite, something your audience knows about:

👍 Citizens were overall less distressed than one might think. [∅]

👍 👎 The citizens were overall less distressed than one might think.

Including *the* in the second sentence seems confusing. After reading that sentence, I wonder, "the citizens of which country or city?" If it's clear from context who's being referred to, *the* is acceptable, but if it's not clear which particular citizens you're talking about, then your reader will be perplexed.[3]

Noncountable, Indefinite Nouns

Note that noncountable nouns do not exist in plural forms. Sometimes noncountable nouns are called "mass nouns," since they refer to something made up of various elements— "mud," "air," "pollution," "traffic," or "water." They lack a definable shape in space and time.

Noncountable nouns use either *the* or no article (∅). They are almost never introduced with *a* or *an*.

Here are some noncountable nouns:

- 👍 *Knowledge* about what these entities were or wanted was nonexistent. [∅]

- 👍 *Management* of our emotions was the key, it seemed. [∅]

- 👍 *The warmth* they felt for each other kept Arpita and Puneet together as a couple. [Definite, so *the* is needed.]

But . . .

- 👍 *Pessimism* prevailed.

- 👍 👎 *A pessimism* prevailed. [This seems to me weaker—less encompassing—than the version without *a*, but it is still acceptable.]

---

[3] I discuss this in more detail in the next chapter's section on "Context-Dependent Article Indefiniteness or Definiteness" (pages 156–62).

☞ The pessimism prevailed. [This won't work as is. To revise, you might say something like, *The pessimism felt by an invaded planet prevailed*. This specifies the pessimism we are talking about, making the noun definite.]

Using *a* prior to the subjects of these preceding sentences (about *knowledge*, *management*, *warmth*, and *pessimism*) communicates the general idea but does so somewhat awkwardly. For example, using *a* with *pessimism* seems to suggest that more will be added: "A pessimism prevailed among all inhabitants of small towns," and more perhaps should be included—maybe an adjective—that helped define that pessimism, as in, "A woeful pessimism prevailed. . . ."

On the other hand, when you talk about a "shovelful of dirt" or a "pail of milk," the noun in question is countable because of the countability of its container. For example, you can't really say "a mud" or "a milk," but *a bucket of mud* or *two pails of milk* are understandable expressions. (*The* bucket of mud or *the* pail of milk [countable, singular, definite] are acceptable if the listener is familiar with that very bucket of mud or pail of milk being referenced.)

A mud, *an air*, *a pollution* make no sense without modifiers, though, such as *a mud pie*, *an air quality issue*, *a dangerous level of pollution*: the modifiers move them into the countable, singular, indefinite category.

Noncountable, Definite Nouns

Here are some sentences where the definite article (*the*) is preferable because the reference is to something more specific and definable than, say, *knowledge*, *management*, or *pessimism*—and also something the audience is familiar with:

- 👍 The shared *ignorance* was a bit alarming.

- 👍 The *hospitality* shown to the aliens was touching and confidence inspiring.

- 👍 The *violence*, though, was foolish: attacking the aliens only caused collateral damage.

Note that in these examples, omitting the article yields sentences that seem a bit chopped off (though marginally acceptable since doing that would make the nouns noncountable and indefinite). The indefinite article (*a*) would yield nonsensical results.

Nouns Either Countable or Noncountable

As you might have guessed, some nouns fit into either category, depending on context. "I am majoring in business" includes a noncountable, indefinite noun, but in the sentence "His business was vandalized last night," the same noun is countable, singular, and definite. Here is Dalgish's explanation of what goes on:

> Just as is the situation with most words, almost any noun can have multiple meanings, some countable, some noncountable. Interestingly, the intended meaning of the noun determines the determiner, so to speak. *Business* has many meanings: one is the noncount meaning "the study of buying, selling, or ripping people off"; another is the countable sense of "a physical place where such activity is conducted," that is, a *place of business*.

Here is how a noun can take *a*, *the*, and then ∅, moving from countable to noncountable:

👍 "There's *a man* in our back yard," Arpita said, looking out the window of the kitchen. [Some man, they don't know who: countable, singular, indefinite.]

👍 Joining her in the kitchen, Puneet brought in a pair of binoculars. "Let's see," he said, peering through the lenses. "*The man* is trying to hold up a sign." [Puneet and Arpita know which man Puneet is looking at through the binoculars; it's now a countable, singular, definite noun.]

👍 It was in fact Garrastazu, who was in the process of unfurling *a* large sign he had made. It read, "*Man* is doomed." "Do you want to go out and tell him that *the* sign should use the word 'Humankind' instead of 'Man'? Or am I going to have to do that?" Puneet asked. "You go," said Arpita.

You can see how the noun starts off as a countable, singular indefinite noun and thus takes the indefinite article, *a*. It's some man, we don't know who. But after he is sort of "known" by both people in the conversation, he becomes *the* man in their backyard. In the last sentence, *Garrastazu*, the man holding the sign, is a singular proper noun, not a class or category. Therefore no article is needed. *A* sign indicates that nothing is yet known about that sign. At the next mention, we know which sign is being referenced, so it becomes *the* sign. "*Man is doomed*" is so general that *Man* is indefinite and is also noncountable; hence it takes ∅ (we can't say *humankinds*).

Interestingly, a typically noncountable noun can morph into being countable. Here how Dalgish puts it:

In informal English, a normally noncountable noun can become a countable noun. "I'll take two sugars with my coffee" means "I'll take two [packets of/teaspoons of/ lumps of sugar]." "Bring two waters and one Coke" means "Bring two [of the designated or understood containers of] water and one [designated or understood container of] Coke." Typically, *sugar* and *water* are noncountable.

You have to figure out if a noun in this category is being used in a countable or noncountable way. Then you should follow the rules for determiner use with that variety of noun.

Postdeterminers

These words occur after a central determiner (such as an article), in order to modify a noun. They include ordinal numbers (first, second, third, and so on), cardinal numbers (one, two, three, and so on), or adjectives. If all three are present, the order is ordinal, cardinal, adjective. The following example follows this order:

👍 *About a third of the 5,000 distressed* residents of Pequa had more than one alien visitor. [*About* is a predeterminer; *a* is a central determiner; *third* is an ordinal number (postdeterminer); *the* is a central determiner; *5,000* is a cardinal number (postdeterminer), and *distressed* is an adjective, also functioning as a postdeterminer. The noun is *residents*.]

Violating Order of Determiners

Note that if you use several determiners, you should try to maintain a definite order. There is some flex to all of this, as you might imagine, since people will understand what you're getting across even if you violate the standard order (it's like the order of adjectives that I discuss earlier). If you violate the typical order of pre-, central, and postdeterminer, you are likely to be veering off into some slang usages, like "The all of it" (which is in fact the title of a novel by Jeannette Haien, perhaps used because the odd determiner order catches our attention), or "Those few scared me" (this might work for some but sounds a little off to me), or "That neither liked." "Neither liked that" is more natural and respects the predeterminer + central determiner order.

When to Use *A* as Opposed to *An*

A is used before words that start with a consonant sound (consonants are *b, c, d, f, g, h, j, k, l, m, n, p, q, r, s, t, v, w, x*, and *z*). *An* is used before words that start with a vowel sound (the vowels are *a, e, i, o, u*, and sometimes *y*). Thus we would have *a car, a bat, a person, a zebra*; but *an idea, an ego, an original thought, an egg*. Words that start with *h* typically use *a* unless the *h* is not pronounced, such as in words like *honest* or *hour*. While these two words start with a written consonant (*h*), they begin with a vowel sound; hence, they require *an*: *an honest dealer*; *an hour*. How about this:

👍 👎 The sudden alien influx was clearly *an historic event* of titanic proportions.

It seems to me that most native speakers would use *a* rather than *an*. But I have seen *an* used before words like *historic*. Either word is acceptable, but you should keep in mind that some readers or listeners would think that *an* before *historic* is slightly pretentious.

8

Varieties of Definiteness, or More Essentials of *The* and *A/An*

I want to focus on a major question I mentioned in the previous chapter: What situations call for the definite article *the*, and what situations require *a/an*? Usually it's fairly easy to tell if a noun is plural, singular, countable, or noncountable, but *definiteness* is much more difficult to ascertain. For example, as figure 1 shows, a common noun that's countable and singular may take *the* or *a/an*. Well, OK, but which? The answer is that it depends entirely on whether the noun is definite or indefinite. This chapter surveys what might be called the varieties of definiteness and offers examples of the kinds of sentences in which these might occur.

A for Singular; *The* for Singular or Plural

To start with a fundamental issue, *a* can only occur prior to singular nouns, while *the* can occur before either singular or plural nouns.

👍 Arpita thought that maybe *a* glass of water would help clear her head. [*The* would be possible here, provided that the audience knew something about Arpita and that particular glass of water. Maybe drinking a glass of water when she felt confused was just a habit of hers that the listener was familiar with, for example.]

👍 Once he got home, Puneet scrolled through all *the* websites he typically consulted.

Collective nouns, which express plurality but take a singular form, though, such as *committee, team, group,* and the like, all may take either *a* or *the.*

Context-Dependent Article Indefiniteness or Definiteness

To review, *a/an* is the *indefinite article,* while *the* is the *definite article. A/an* refers to something that's generalized and nonspecific: *a car, a president, an idea, a historic event.* Which car, president, idea, event? We don't know. It's nonspecific. *The,* by contrast, always refers to something quite specific and/or known to your audience. *The president, the invasion, the sudden alien influx.* A noun becomes definite in a context in which BOTH the speaker and the listener know about the noun being referred to.

👍 Arpita said, "*The* aliens in everyone's house are somehow fitting in." [Definite, specific, known to both speaker and listener.]

👍 Puneet responded, "They also seem to be residing on *the* street." [*The* is needed before *street* since it is definite, a place both of them are familiar with.]

👍 "Well, they are definitely on *the* street where we live," Arpita noted. [Again, a known, definite place.]

☞ "And in house, too." [Puneet probably should say, in *our* house or in *the* house, though the expression *in house* does appear in some situations where it means *internal*. It does not work here, however.]

👍 "I think I saw *an* alien in *a* tree, too," Arpita pointed out. [Two indefinite uses: some alien, an unknown one, and a tree, also nonspecified—not sure where it is.]

👍 "Yes, there was one in *the* alder tree," Puneet replied. [A very specific tree that they both know about, an alder, probably on or near their property; hence, a definite one.]

👍 It was *a* strange situation. [Again, indefinite; no one is sure how strange it is, what will happen as a result of the alien invasion, how people will respond.]

👍 It was *the* strangest situation that anyone had ever encountered" [This is much more precise and defined than the previous; hence *the* is used; *strangest* particularizes the situation.]

Again, whether to choose *a/an* or *the* often depends on what your intended audience knows about the context of a given situation. If your audience is familiar with the noun, use *the*; if not, you cannot use *the*.

👍 *The* alien invasion was making life difficult for everyone.

👍 In fact, *the* proliferation of guns and weaponry was destroying large swaths of American cities and towns. People would shoot at *the* aliens, who were unaffected, and *the* bullets would pass through them only to do damage to something or someone else.

👍 Gun manufacturers ramped up production and sales skyrocketed as Americans went on *a* weapons-buying spree. *The* spree was short-lived, though. [The reason the first weapons-buying spree uses an indefinite article is that this is new news. The second *spree* takes the definite article because that spree, introduced in the prior sentence, is one that the audience is now sort of familiar with.]

Here is another situation in which the article use moves from indefinite to definite:

👍 A local police officer arrested *a* man on Woodmead Avenue following *a* motor vehicle accident near the public library late Saturday night. Authorities had no details about *the* incident, but *the* driver claimed to be veering to miss hitting *an* alien puddle person. *A* local resident said that *the* police handcuffed *the* inebriated man after he crawled out of his battered BMW at 1:00 a.m.

The sentence starts with the assumption that the listener knows nothing about the *officer* or *man* or *motor vehicle involved*. Since the listener does not yet know these nouns, *a* (the indefinite article) is needed. Once these nouns are established early in the sentence as the nouns involved in the situation, the writer knows that with subsequent mentions, the listener/reader knows which *police officer*, *driver*, and *motor vehicle* the sentence is referring to. Thus at second and later mentions, the definite article *the* is correct.

This "first mention/second mention" concept is the way all human language discourse progresses, from the unknown to the known, from the indefinite to the definite. Dalgish notes that it's why many fairy tales start with "Once upon a time, there was *a* beautiful princess. . . ." Subsequent mentions of *princess* will be definite: "The princess was very sad and lonely." After the first mention, the writer knows that the listener/reader can easily "figure out" which princess is being discussed.

Definiteness When Referring to the Culturally Expected

This is a subset of the previous category. You should use the definite article, *the*, with a noun that refers to something that everyone is familiar with and exists as a singular, unique entity, such as *the sun, the moon, the Declaration of Independence, the deeps, the Lord, the Internet, the ground*, or even expressions like *the local bully, the corner deli*. (This also covers slang or idiomatic expressions, such as "He got *the hook*," or "He will be given *the chair*" [that is, he was executed in the electric chair].) *The morning, the afternoon, the evening*, and other time expressions, such as *the future* or *the past* also require *the*, as do references to time periods such as *the sixties* or *the late nineteenth century*. (No article, though with *God*, which is usually ∅, except in polytheistic contexts when *god* would not be capitalized, as in "Some people think that the god Poseidon punished Odysseus a little too harshly.")

If the writer can safely assume that the noun is part of the listener's culturally expected environment, *the* is used. In a sentence like "Arpita, did you let *the* dog out?" the use of *the* is appropriate because the partners both know or can figure out which dog they mean. The same holds with the sentence, "They recently bought *a* new house. *The* kitchen was too small, but the living room was huge. But overall they loved *the* house." *A* is used before *new house* because it's the first mention and we know nothing about it: it's indefinite. *The* is used in second mention. We use *the* before *kitchen* and before *living room* because the cultural assumption shared by speaker and listener is that all houses typically have a kitchen and a living room.

In addition, ordinary things that are part of our shared environment will take a *the* when we know the items. Thus, *the* occurs in expressions about common items that we encounter on a daily basis, as in "*the* teapot just boiled," "*the* mail came," "*the* toilet is running again," "*the* sugar bowl is empty." In addition, *the* gives a sense of something present and actually happening, as in "*the* problem at hand"; "*the* game on TV"; "*the* Christmas season is here." These are all simply defined or identified, so *the* is the right article.

The is also used before the titles of various people such as "*the* president," "*the* mayor," or, in some situations, "*the* boss." *The* is the determiner of choice when a person's title precedes a prepositional phrase, as in "*the* Speaker of the House," "*the* justice of the peace." *The* is also used with an adjective to make up a phrase that names someone or something, such as "*the* White House," "Æthelred *the* Unready" and "Bolesław *the* Bold" (medieval kings of England and Poland, respectively), "Winnie *the* Pooh," or even "Stan *the* Man" (Stan Musial, the baseball great). Similarly, *the* is used prior to the nicknames of some famous persons, such as "*the* Great One" (Michael Jackson), "*the* Boss" (Bruce Springsteen), "*the* Schnozz" (Jimmy Durante).

You can sometimes drop the noun after the use of an article: "translated from *the* Sanskrit" drops the noun "language"; "meet you at *the* Empire State" drops "building"; "check *the* unabridged" drops "dictionary." It is important to note, though, that this use of *the* can occur only when the speaker or writer knows that the listener or reader can easily figure out the dropped noun. Again, whether or not you can use *the* depends on how much the audience can be assumed to know.

Place Names Using Definite Article

Many singular proper nouns require the definite article. Here is a partial list:

the United States

the USSR

the Mississippi River

the Antarctic

the high plains

the Rocky Mountains

the Alps

the Pacific, the Atlantic

the Black Sea

the Eiffel Tower

the Chrysler Building

the Statue of Liberty

the Washington Monument

Here are some suggestions that Dalgish has worked out for proper nouns designating place names:

- If it ends in *s and* the word looks or sounds like a plural, it takes *the*. (However, Queens, Dallas, Des Moines, and many other place names do *not* sound like plurals, so ∅; some that end in an *s*-sound take *the*, like *the* Bronx [originally the Broncks], while others don't, like Halifax or Appomattox.)

- If it's an abbreviation of anything that in its full form has a *the*, it takes *the*: *the* United States, *the* US.

- Use before name + river/ocean/sea (bodies of water) or the names of mountain ranges: *the* Baltic Sea, *the* Indian Ocean, *the* Nile; *the* Andes, *the* Adirondacks; *the* Himalayas.

- Use before well-known common nouns include buildings, towers, monuments: *the* Lincoln Memorial; *the* Washington Monument; *the* Gateway Arch.

- Also use prior to place names with *of* in them: *the People's Republic of China*; *the Isle of Wight*; *the Garden of Eden*; *the* Leaning Tower of Pisa, *the* City of Brotherly Love.

Definiteness: Superlatives and the Remarkable

The definite article is also used in situations where you want to call attention to something specific and/or striking. For example, *the* is used before adjectives like *same, best, worst, fastest, strongest, utmost,* and other superlatives.

👍 It was *the* worst time he had ever lived through, Puneet realized. [Countable, singular, definite.]

In a similar way, *the* sometimes indicates and singles out something that is exceptional, "To Sherlock Holmes she is always *the* woman" (3), Sir Arthur Conan Doyle's story "A Scandal in Bohemia" begins. People frequently use the definite article this way.

The is used with a plural noun when you are trying to establish a paradigm case or proverbial example: "As unbeatable as *the* 1927 Yankees," "As decadent as *the* Romans under Nero's rule."

Definiteness of Adjectives Functioning as Nouns

As mentioned in the chapter on adjectives (page 118), *the* appears before adjectives that are functioning as nouns (nominal adjectives): "*The* wicked watcheth *the* righteous" (Psalms 37:32).

👍 It was a year when *the* astounding had become commonplace. [Noncountable, definite.]

"*The meek* shall inherit the earth" and "Only *the strong* survive" are common expressions, though they seem to have opposite meanings. "Ernest, *the rich* are different from you and me," F. Scott Fitzgerald supposedly told Hemingway.[1]

Definiteness and Names of Plants/Animals

Here is one of the miscellaneous uses of *the*. Use *the* before names of living creatures (except humans) and of precious stones. These following examples are of generalized nouns expressing some well-known or widely accepted information

---

[1]   Hemingway supposedly replied, "Yeah, they have more money."

about the nouns: "*The* octopus is much misunderstood," "*The* archaeopteryx is the earliest known bird," "*The* redwood tree is gigantic," "*The* diamond is the hardest natural substance," "*The* forsythia are blooming," "*The* cobra strikes with astonishing speed," "*The* cat is fey." (The indefinite article also works in sentences such as "*A* cat is fey," or "*A* cobra strikes with astonishing speed." If you want to pluralize, you can drop the article and use the plural verb ["Cats are fey"]). I note here that a plant/tree has to have a certain size or prominence before it can be used with the definite article. Usually they will take ∅ and the plural ("Crotons are high maintenance"; "Aloe vera plants are easy to maintain") rather than definite article and singular.

Definiteness/Indefiniteness and Numbers

In terms of indicating numbers or frequency, *the* is often used. For example, use *the* with an ordinal number: "I've done this for *the* tenth time." *Tenth* is a postdeterminer, which occurs after the article, you probably recall. *The* is also used with *by* to mean *each and every*, as in "He is paid *by the* day" (singular, countable; definite).

By contrast, *a/an* can mean *each*, *any*, or *every*:

👍 Some workers are paid on a day-by-day basis. [We don't know specifics of the actual pay; *day-by-day basis* is thus indefinite, countable (*bases* being the plural), and singular.]

👍 Puneet sees *a* problem and wants to solve it. That's just the way he is made. [Countable, singular, indefinite.]

The indefinite article, *a*, can also mean *the same as* or *equivalent to*, and typically occurs after a form of the *to be* verb such as *is* or *was:*

👍 President Akbaliatuk was *a* compromiser, at least in the minds of some people.

👍 Puneet was *a* relentless seeker of knowledge.

The *to be* verbs establish the equivalences in both of these sentences, which take the form of noun phrase + *to be* verb + complement. In all these situations, singular noun forms that are indefinite require the *a/an*.

Some expressions, ones that involve numerals in relation to non-numerals, such as *five times a week, two hundred dollars an hour, five at-bats a game* also take the indefinite article: the *a* is equivalent to *per*. Note, too, that the indefinite article appears in many predeterminers that act as quantifiers: *a few, a little, a lot, a bunch of, a portion.*

Definiteness and Signaling of Role-Playing or Specialness

The sometimes conveys additional meanings, suggesting a true significance to the noun they modify. For example, use *the* in expressions that metaphorically (or literally) refer to theatrical archetypes: "plays *the* fool," "plays *the* diva," "plays *the* ingenue," "plays *the* straight man," "acts *the* part." *The* can be used when there is a noun phrase in apposition to the noun, as in "*the* performer Lady Gaga," "*the* film star Sandra Bullock." (These are countable, singular, and definite, so they follow the usual pattern.)

The definite article can also emphasize the importance of someone or something: "Are you *the* Sandra Bullock?" I would explain this by suggesting that in sentences like this, the proper noun (Sandra Bullock) is being treated like a common, noncountable, definite noun: the name is being silently modified by "famous" or something similar: "Are you the famous actress Sandra Bullock?"

The *the* in the names of some famous works of art is a little less explicable. We have, on one hand, names like *The Mona Lisa, The Pietà, The Starry Night, The Scream, The Garden of Earthly Delights*. Some famous paintings include an *A* in their title: *A Cotton Office in New Orleans, A Bar at the Folies Bergère, A Friend in Need*. By contrast, no article is used with *Guernica, American Gothic, Satan Devouring His Son*, or *Nighthawks*.[2]

Definiteness That Will Be Explained Later On in the Sentence

Dalgish provides another important category. He writes, "*The* will occur before a noun when it's followed by a phrase or clause that serves to limit that noun's scope, or specify that scope more exactly: '*the* walls **that** seemed to close in on him,' '*the* strong **of** will,' '*the* means **to** grow.' As with place names, the *that*-, *of*-, or *to*-phrase demands a *the*. When immediately defined or narrowed down, *the* is being used to say, 'I'm about to signal or define it; hold your horses.'"

---

[2]   Since many artwork names are translations, it's difficult to draw any firm conclusions about their article use. Still, more research is needed on this matter.

Articles Used in Reference to Physical Ailments

To briefly venture beyond the basics, *the* is used with parts of the body, as with "the brain," "the heart," "the spine," in the absence of other central determiners, such as possessives ("your brain," "her heart").

Medical or physical conditions require various determiners, depending on the disease: some require *a/an*, some *the*, some ∅. We talk about people *presenting with cancer, contracting monkeypox, having ALS, catching the flu, coming down with a sore throat, in bed with a fever*. I spend a little extra time on this because article use with ailments and conditions might provide insight into article use in general.

The indefinite article (*a/an*) is used most often in conjunction with conditions that can be one of many possible types within a much broader category: *a cold, a stye, a tumor, an aneurysm*. The indefinite article reflects the indefiniteness of the condition. All of these conditions include a wide range of ailments—for example, some tumors are malignant, some benign. Some are operable, others not. Some are big, some small. Colds are quite common and caused by any number of viruses, some more dangerous than others. Aneurysms come in all sorts of shapes and sizes, at a variety of locations in the body, and in all degrees of severity.

Note that if you have an adjective that helps describe the ailment, you will almost always need the indefinite article prior to that adjective, as in *a sore* throat, *a broken* wrist, *a brain* tumor, *a slipped* disc. Putting the article there makes the ailment less general, a specific one of many possible variants. The adjective follows the central determiner and functions as a postdeterminer.

When *the* is the sole determiner, it indicates that both audience and speaker know something about the ailment, and/or that it is special or exceptionally prevalent: *the coronavirus, the plague, the omicron variant, the flu, the pox, the measles.*

The zero article (∅), that is, no article at all, is used in situations where the ailment is specific and almost always serious, even though it might be part of a large enough category to seem to warrant an indefinite article. *Cancer* usually does not take an article; the name of the disease is usually narrowed down by an adjectival determiner: *pancreatic cancer, lung cancer, breast cancer.* With other ailments sometimes one name for it takes one determiner and another name takes another. For example, *influenza* never takes a determiner, but the same disease, when called *the flu* or *the grippe*, takes the definite article.

Diseases and conditions named after people also take ∅: *Parkinson's disease, Sjögren's syndrome, Dupuytren's contracture, Alzheimer's disease, Paget's disease.* Long and complex disease names also usually take ∅: *pneumonia, diphtheria, dysentery, tuberculosis, syphilis, coccidioidomycosis*, and many others fall into this category and are treated like ordinary singular proper nouns.

Names of diseases that sound plural sometimes take the definite article, sometimes ∅. We usually say *the measles, the mumps, the runs,* though the article can be dropped in all but the latter example. However, we never say *the hemorrhoids, the rabies, the shingles, the hives,* or *the rickets.* The reason for this is that these five last-mentioned conditions are not true plurals. Huddleston and Pullum note, "The existence of the singular form *shingle* helps give *shingles* the appearance of a plural form, but this appearance is misleading: it is singular" (346). The singular *shingle* has nothing to do with the disease but refers to tiles on a roof or a sign board (as in *hanging your shingle*). *Shingles*, aka herpes zoster, is a *pseudo-plural*.

The rule for diseases differs slightly from the rule mentioned earlier for proper noun place names—that is, if it ends in *s and* looks or sounds plural, use *the*, as in *the Grand Tetons* or *the Andes*. For example, *rickets*, *shingles*, *hives*, and *rabies* all end in *s* and all look or sound plural, yet they never require an article. Disease names that require an article have to end in an *s*, but the disease they refer to also has to have something conceptually plural about it. What might be called *symptom plurality* seems to count when deciding whether an article is needed. We use the definite article with some diseases whose plural form indicates a multiplicity or repetition of symptoms: the hiccups is characterized by "involuntary *contractions* of the diaphragm . . . [which] may persist for months" (Mayo Clinic, my emphasis). The measles presents as hundreds of blotches or blisters. The mumps often involves the swelling of both salivary glands. (*The runs* is very much a plural.)

Decompression sickness or Caisson disease—*the bends*—is a condition whose name looks plural. Huddleston and Pullum claim that as a disease name, *the bends* is "not systematically related to the [form] without the *s*" (346). I disagree. The plurality of the disease's informal name, *the bends*, stems from the fact that people afflicted with it, usually deep-sea divers who surface too quickly, cannot straighten their joints. Their joints are all *bent*: they have a bend in the knees, elbows, ankles, wrists. Hence, the many bent joints yielded the name *the bends*. So I would call *the bends* a true plural, not a pseudo-plural. It always requires *the*.

Here, in short form, are three barest-essential rules for using *the*, *a/an*, or neither (∅):

1. *The* is used when something is somehow particular and/or special, known to both the speaker and reader, or culturally familiar.
2. *A/an* is used for more general, nonspecific references of various kinds, and at first mention of a noun unknown to the audience.
3. Proper nouns (names) do not take determiners, unless the names are pluralized (*the* United States), or they are offered in singular form as one of a class or category (*a Ford* is easy to fix), or are names of rivers, oceans, or mountain ranges.

What I have presented here is only a limited and general sketch of how English uses determiners. You will have to seek out a more comprehensive grammar in order to run down all the complexities of this aspect of English and the many other specific uses of the definite and indefinite articles. But keep in mind that mastering determiner use will increase both your own confidence with the language and the confidence that others have in you.

PART FIVE
Clarity

When you need to communicate in writing, and especially when you need to communicate something complex, you need to make sure that you are expressing yourself clearly. When we speak, we can simply insert pauses and stresses where needs be, "upspeak" when uncertain, shout when agitated. But in written English, we don't have those options. We do, however, have punctuation, which clarifies as it helps to convey our message.

Our written language is full of pauses and stops, and each of these carries some element of your meaning. We have the short pause of the comma, the interruptive pause of the em-dash, the more definite, longer pause of the period. And what of the semicolon and colon? How long a pause do they require? And how do we use punctuation to stress what's important, or downplay what's incidental?

In this part, I will look at punctuation marks and show how each is typically used to increase clarity and help you convey some of the subtleties of your message.

9

Semicolons, Hyphens, and Other Baffling Punctuation Marks

To begin with what most of you probably know, at the end of each sentence, you need to have some mark of punctuation, such as a period, a question mark, or an exclamation point. If you use a fragment for dramatic effect, you need to punctuate that as a sentence. Like this? Yes. Like that.

In other languages, such as Spanish, questions or exclamations have end marks but are also marked at the start of the sentence with an inverted question mark or exclamation point:

👍 *¿Quién sabe lo que está pasando?*

👍 Who knows what's going on?

In Polish, the word *Czy* may introduce a question that is answered by yes or/no. In French, *n'est-ce pas* may be appended to a sentence in order to mark a question. In English, to signal a question we may open with words like *which*, *how*, *when*, *where*, *whose*, *what*, *why*. However, sometimes it's not evident that we are exclaiming something or asking a direct question until that last punctuation mark, making that end-mark quite important.

I should note that today, the exclamation point is experiencing a sort of renascence, particularly in electronic communications of various kinds. In fact, in text messages, omitting the exclamation point is downright rude. But in formal written English, one should generally avoid using the exclamation point. Several writers on the subject contend that we are allowed only one exclamation point in our formal written English—just one per lifetime!

Semicolons

A semicolon looks like this → ;

The semicolon is indeed one of the mysteries of the modern world. But it need not be. Cecelia Watson has authored an excellent book about semicolons, called *Semicolon: The Past, Present, and Future of a Misunderstood Mark*. As to the use of this curious mark of punctuation, some people unfortunately use the notoriously unreliable "pause rule"—namely, if a pause is longer than that of a comma, a semicolon is used. Another incorrect conceptualization is that you should use a semicolon when you can't decide between a comma and a period. Nope. Indecision never dictates punctuation.

Semicolons are used in two ways:

1. The first, most common use of the semicolon is to signal the start of a new main clause. A main clause, you recall, is just a full sentence: a noun phrase + verb phrase + tense. It can stand on its own. Sometimes you will want to attach one main clause to another, creating a closer relationship between the two main clauses than you'd have if you kept them as separate sentences.

   Theoretically, you can string together any number of main clauses, but in general, you should use a semicolon only when joining main clauses that have some connection to each other, some tight relationship that you think is important to emphasize—cause-effect or a sequence of events, as in *first this*; *then that*. The linguist Susan J. Behrens offers sound advice here: "I like to tell students that the semi-colon is perfectly designed: half comma, half period. The period part means you are separating two independent clauses; the comma part signals that the two clauses convey related ideas" (164).

👍 President Akbaliatuk had the option of declaring war or martial law; showing remarkable restraint, he chose the latter.

👍 Much of the country's current problem revolved around the use of personal weapons such as firearms or explosive devices; these, under martial law, would be confiscated.

Connected to this usage is the slightly unusual situation in which the verb of the second main clause is dropped out, the rationale being that the first main clause's verb is implied:

👍 Universities all went to online instruction; schools, to early vacation.

👍 Gun owners loved their rifles; some, their shotguns; still others, their semiautomatics.

As mentioned earlier, when they are used to join main clauses, conjunctive adverbs like *however*, *therefore*, or *for example* require a semicolon before them:

👍 Puneet and Arpita still had to work; however, they spent more and more time working from home.

☞ The newspaper was a daily, therefore, it required a lot more work from its employees than it ever had. [Semicolon needed prior to *therefore*.]

2. The semicolon may also be used to separate elements in a list that is long and in which at least one of the main elements contains internal punctuation, namely, commas.

👍 Places such as Little Rock, Arkansas; Laramie, Wyoming; Columbus, Ohio; and Miami, Florida, all resisted the confiscation of personal weapons.

👍 The National Rifle Association argued that guns were crucial, even necessary for personal protection; that confiscating guns was a clearly a Fascist, authoritarian, and damaging policy; and, worst of all, that the president was violating the Second Amendment.

These lists might be confusing if they used only commas to separate their various elements, though I think the second sentence would still work with only commas since it maintains a strict parallelism.[1]

Colons

A colon looks like this → :

The colon is used in several conventional ways, by which I mean that it's come to function in a certain way just through longstanding practice.

---

[1] I discuss parallelism in chapter 11.

Conventional usages include a colon in time expressions, such as 9:00 p.m. (but 2100 hours); in URLs (*https:*); after the salutation in a formal letter, and as a way to introduce a some quoted material:

👍 The president was receiving many letters such as the following:

Dear President Akbaliatuk:

It has come to my attention that you are in the process of terrorizing and controlling the American populace in the name of dealing with an alien invasion that you have publicly called a hoax. . . .

👍 His spokesperson responded as follows:

Dear Citizen:

Thank you for your inquiry. The president called the invasion a "hoax" in the sense that he recognized aliens had landed but maintained they were peaceful. He demanded weapons be confiscated so that the aliens weren't slaughtered and people were not inadvertently injured by the many weapons being discharged. Here are the president's very words: "Guns need to be confiscated in order to save the lives of many Americans."

Note that in an informal letter or e-mail, say, one to a friend or close associate, a comma rather than a colon follows the salutation.

In general, the colon introduces something elaborating on a previously mentioned idea, or introduces something that repeats, using other words, what precedes it. It can be used to introduce a list or any item that you have singled out for special emphasis. It often sets off a closing appositive, the idea being that such a construction gives the sentence a resounding impact:

👍 For many people, it seemed that the puddles that had entered their homes were pleasant companions: alien pets.

👍 In fact, people would dip their fingers into the puddles and feel a strange, wondrous sensation of relaxation and relief: an entrance into another dimension.

Theoretically, you can have a complete sentence after a colon, such as (to modify the last example sentence), "it was like an entrance into another dimension." Bryan A. Garner has, as usual, particularly good advice here. He says a colon

> may link two separate clauses or phrases by indicating a step forward from the first to the second: the step may be from an introduction to a main theme, from a cause to an effect, from a general statement to a particular instance, or from a premise to a conclusion. (747)

In other words, it implies a slightly stronger, tighter connection between the first and the second clause than if a semicolon were used.

With the exception of its use in a time expression, URL, or letter salutation, you should probably have a full sentence (main clause) preceding the colon. You don't, for example, want to place a colon between subject and verb. Rarely do you want to use a colon after a *to be* verb (*am, is, are, were, was, being, been, be*), though I note that this particular rule is frequently violated. One could argue that using a colon after a fragment is a stylistic choice. Maybe this is true. But is it the best choice?

👎 In short, like much of the populace, Puneet and
  Arpita were: amazed by the aliens. [No colon needed.]

One additional prohibition, possibly more stylistic than grammar-based, is the following: you shouldn't use more than one colon in a sentence, as this can potentially confuse readers. (This does not apply to the colons in time expressions or URLs.)

The portion of the sentence after the colon should start with a capital letter in several situations (I am here simply presenting the MLA style manual's suggestions [Altreuter]):

1. If the word after the colon is typically capitalized;

2. If the material following the colon is composed of more than one sentence;

3. If the material following the colon elaborates a rule or principle, or poses a direct question.

  👍 When people consulted their nail-mons, the first
    thing they saw was always the same: President
    Akbaliatuk going on about something to do with
    the aliens. [Capitalized word after the colon.]

  👍 Puneet faced several problems: He was unsure what
    he should write about. He did not know what he
    and Arpita should do about the aliens in the house.
    And he had no idea what this whole situation would
    morph into. [More than one sentence.]

  👍 As the famous baseball player Yogi Berra would say,
    the situation could be summed up in one word:

"You never know." [A rule or principle. (Note the clever illogicality of the Berra-ism.)]

👍 There was only one problem that everyone had: What should humans do now? [Direct question.]

Hyphens and Dashes

There are three kinds of dash marks: the hyphen, the en-dash, and the em-dash. Probably the most important thing to remember is the following: don't confuse a hyphen and an em-dash.

Hyphens

A hyphen looks like this → -

A hyphen suggests a hyphenated word, a two-part, specific concept, if you will, while a dash separates one word, phrase, or thought from another.

👍 He told many audiences—and here, he was being both honest and humble—that he didn't know what to do and was just going from day to day with the alien issue. [Em-dashes used correctly here to indicate an inserted phrase.]

👎 President Akbaliatuk's greatest desire-his ultimate goal-was to retain power and influence. [Em-dashes, not hyphens, are needed here; as it stands, *desire-his* and *goal-was* sound like separate noun phrases.]

The use of hyphens is remarkably complex. Hyphens are used in the following ways. (Again, I am drawing from the *MLA Handbook*, ninth edition, as well as from the *Chicago Manual of Style*): for the general form of these guidelines.)

1. Hyphenate multiple-word adjectives that occur *before the noun,* including adverbs such as *well, better, ill, best.*

   👍 It was an **ill-prepared** population that the aliens encountered.

   👍 **Well-known** writer Puneet Tagore published some articles attempting to explain the situation, though his work was not as widely read as that of other journalists.

But . . .

   👎 The **most-popular** writing on the subject tended to be sensationalist. [*Less, least, more,* and *most* do not require hyphens in compound adjectives before a noun.]

   👎 **Happily-married** to another writer, Arpita Tagore, Puneet often asked his wife to collaborate with him on writing projects. [Adverbs that end in -*ly,* even when they form compounds, don't require a hyphen.]

   👎 They had met at a **high-school** reunion. [No hyphen needed since *high school* is a common compound that occurs in an unhyphenated form.]

   👎 The **Asian-American** population was blamed and targeted by domestic terrorists after the invasion. [No hyphen needed when the adjective is formed from two nouns. Just use Asian American.]

2. When you want to combine a number with a regular noun form.

   👍 It was a **ten-hour** journey by car to the capital, but Puneet thought it might be worthwhile for him to go there.

👍 He seemed to have a **twentieth-century** sensibility when it came to travel, so he spent a lot more time in his car rather than on a superfast maglev train.

3. When you have an adjectival prepositional phrase prior to noun.

    👍 The couple's **on-point** reporting had gained them some notoriety.

But . . .

    👍 The couple's reporting was **on point**. [No hyphen needed when the adjectival prepositional phrase *follows* the noun.]

4. When leaving out the hyphen distorts your meaning.

    👍 They were distressed, though, when the woman in the **grass-green** skirt knocked on their door. She said she was from the CIA. [Without the hyphen, the reader would initially imagine a woman in the grass.]

5. When you use what are called "suppressed" words.

    👍 The CIA agent asked Arpita, "Are you **first**-, **second**-, or **third-generation** Americans?"

    👍 Arpita replied, "We are **pre**- and **post-invasion** Americans, which should be all that matters at this point."

6. When you employ various prefixes such as *ex*- (meaning *former*), *self*-, *all*-; with the suffix *-elect*; between a variety of prefixes that come before a proper noun; and with single-letter prefixes, such as *T-shirt* or *F-word*.

7. When you name fractions, as in *three-fourths full,
two-thirds of an inning.*

8. When you have two modifiers that, connected, would
smush together letters that could be easily confused:

👍 Puneet and Arpita wore their profession in a
protective, **shell-like** manner. [With no hyphen, this
would be *shelllike*.]

👍 Essentially, Puneet and Arpita were **semiindependent** contractors. The CIA agent did not like
this designation and informed the couple that they
would have to be interrogated. [*Semiindependent* is a
little hard to process with the repeated vowel. Having
two *i*'s in a row won't work, but having two *e*'s in a row
is acceptable: *reemphasize, reelect,* and *reenact* are
acceptable but also can take hyphens. You just need to
be consistent within a single piece of writing.]

9. Numerals of more than one word need to be spelled
out and hyphenated, though numerals over a hundred
do not need this treatment:

👍 Arpita held up her hands. "Great. I've just videoed
all this and sent it with a message to **twenty-five**
media outlets. They will disperse it to another 757,
give or take." [By contrast, round numbers, like two
hundred or five thousand, should be spelled out.]

10. When used adjectivally, numbers that are joined to
words require a hyphen:

👍 The agent pulled a **six-inch-long knife** out of her
handbag. Then, she put it back and walked to her car.
Arpita included this in her video.

11. MLA also recommends a hyphen before an adjective that precedes a compound adjective like *thirteenth-century*: *early-thirteenth-century architecture*. Chicago Manual style says that the hyphen after *early* is optional. MLA prohibits hyphens in foreign expressions like *ad hoc*, but *The New Yorker* uses a hyphen in this situation. Sorry if that sounds overwhelming. Styles vary.

I should note here that the major "styles" of writing are dictated by what field you are working in or writing for. They don't agree about every detail of punctuation, reference form, or usage. MLA (Modern Language Association) style is used by language and literature disciplines; APA (American Psychological Association) style is employed by professionals in the social and natural sciences; AP (Associated Press) style is used by journalists (though *The New York Times* and *The New Yorker* have their own styles); *The Chicago Manual of Style* is the guide for most academic book publishers in the humanities and social sciences.

The En-Dash

An en-dash looks like this → –

En-dashes are used to indicate page ranges (as in "pages 23–45") and also in the slightly unusual situation where you want a modifier to apply to an entire phrase rather than to just the first word:

👍 In this **post–alien invasion America**, it was unclear how and if people had to change their routines or lives. [En-dash modifies *alien invasion America*, not just *alien*.]

👍 Puneet wondered if they were experiencing what was essentially **pre–World War III**. [Note than an en-dash (–), not a hyphen, is used here since *pre* is modifying not just *World* but *World War III*. This is both a *Chicago Manual of Style* as well as an MLA rule, by the way.]

In some styles, the en-dash indicates opposition, as in the *Eurasia–Ukraine war* or the *good–evil conflict*. Check your discipline's style handbook on the use of the en-dash. The en-dash is a little bit of an outlier among dashes, I fear: rules vary, and different style manuals use it in different ways.

The Em-Dash

An em-dash looks like this → —

Much more familiar and frequently used are em-dashes, and most styles agree about when and where to use them. Em-dashes draw attention to a word or phrase inserted in the middle or at the end of a sentence. Two hyphens, no spaces, is how these are formed on a typewriter. However, many writers, following British or AP style of the em-dash, use a single hyphen or en-dash with spaces on either side. More typically, in the United States, the em-dash is longer than the hyphen or en-dash, and is smashed right up against the words it is placed between:

👍 Meanwhile, the vast majority of the **populace— including Puneet and Arpita**—were unable to agree on what exactly the aliens were like.

👎 👍 Meanwhile, the vast majority of the populace– including Puneet and Arpita–were unable to agree on what exactly the aliens were like. [The sentence uses en-dashes, but you want em-dashes. British and AP styles accept the sentence as is.]

👍 At first, the aliens looked like puddles, **but then— after they had lodged themselves in people's homes**—they took on a variety of shapes.

Note that you have the choice in sentences such as the preceding ones to use em-dashes, parentheses, or commas to set off the internal phrase. How do you choose, though? The late Russell Baker, who wrote for *The New York Times*, is worth quoting on this issue:

> Warning! Use sparingly. The dash SHOUTS. Parentheses whisper. Shout too often, people stop listening; whisper too much, people become suspicious of you. The dash creates a dramatic pause to prepare for an expression needing strong emphasis.
>
> Parentheses help you pause quietly to drop some chatty information not vital to your story.

On the other hand, if you choose neither dashes nor parentheses, but prefer to use only commas to set off a phrase or clause, that's neither shouting nor whispering; it's just (to continue the metaphor) a normal tone of voice.

Parentheses

Parentheses are used to insert added additional information that's not crucial to the message you're trying to get across. They are also used for in-text citation, as I have used them throughout this book. These generally occur in pairs, though sometimes people will use a single parenthesis after a number: 5). (If you have parentheses inside of parentheses, alternate the curved parentheses with square brackets [like this]). Brackets are also used when you need to insert some clarifying material into a quotation. And one more thing: never use a comma before a parenthesis.

Quotation Marks

Quotation marks (or *quote marks*, a shortened form now widely accepted, though some grammarians maintain that *quote* is a verb, not an adjective or noun) indicate that you are taking someone else's words directly from a printed or online source and reproducing them in your written work. You must include these marks to indicate you are using someone else's material; if you do not, you are plagiarizing, which is one of the cardinal sins of writing.[2]

In addition, quote marks are used to represent dialogue— that is, the spoken words of someone, real or fictional. If you are representing speech, and one speaker continues for more than a paragraph, you should end only the last paragraph of that person's utterance on a closing quote mark. However, each paragraph should begin with an opening quote mark, indicating a continuation of speech. In addition, with each change of speaker (a situation that typically occurs only in fiction, when you are representing a conversation), you need to start a new paragraph.

In US English, you should use double quote marks, "like this." British English uses single quote marks as the first

---

[2]   "Patch writing"—a practice in which a writer grabs a sentence here, a sentence there, a paraphrase here, a paraphrase there, and patches them all together into a supposedly original document—is not something I condone or encourage. Do remember, too, that all material generated by an AI like ChatGPT needs to be treated like quotation.

option, 'like this'. Note that the previous sentence shows British style of both single quote marks and punctuation after them. In American English, the period goes inside the quote marks, "like this." Commas go inside as well. Question marks and exclamation points go inside, if what you are quoting is a question or exclamation. If your sentence in which the quote appears is the question or exclamation, then you would put the end punctuation after the quote marks.

Another interesting feature of the quotation is that if you have a quote inside a quote, you need to switch to single quote marks. And for a quote inside a quote inside a quote, you go back to double:

> 👍 Puneet reported, "I was talking to our neighbor, Garrastazu, and he said, 'We need to find a way to kill these things.' I replied, 'Why? The media has deemed them "largely harmless,"' and he just stared at me."

You probably want to keep your quotes inside quotes inside quotes to a minimum.

If you have to indicate a page reference of some kind, you will need to follow the style manual employed by your discipline. Some require the author's name and the date of publication, along with the page number. Some want to include "page" or "p." before that number; other styles prohibit that. And punctuation within these parenthetical in-text citations varies from field to field.

Slash Marks

Slash marks are used when you want to suggest alternative words or phrases, such as in *yes/no questions* or *and/or* constructions. They also indicate line breaks in poetry unless the lines are set off from the rest of your text. If you quote more than four lines, set them off in this manner, with no quotation marks needed:

> Two roads diverged in a yellow wood
> And sorry I could not travel both
> And be one traveler, long I stood
> And looked down one as long as I could
> To where it bent in the undergrowth (Frost 103)

For four lines or fewer, here is how slash marks might be used for continuing the opening of Robert Frost's poem "The Road Not Taken": "Then took the other, as just as fair, / And having perhaps the better claim, / Because it was grassy and wanted wear" (Frost 103). Note that there are spaces before and after the slash marks. Two forward slashes (//) indicate a stanza break.

Slash marks also occur in URLs, but you need to note the distinction between a forward slash and a backslash. If you imagine the slash mark as being a stick image of a human, the forward slash is of a human leaning forward or to the right (/), while the backslash is of a human leaning back or to the left (\). The backslash is reserved for computer coding and is not used in regular prose.

Apostrophes

Apostrophes, which look a little like a "high comma" (or a "flying comma"), are used in contractions, in some plurals, and in most possessive forms.

Apostrophes in Contractions

Contractions are used to shorten verbs, usually in their negative forms. It indicates omission of one or more letters:

should not → *shouldn't*

could not → *couldn't*

will not → *won't*

cannot → *can't*

I shall or *I will* → *I'll*

I shall not → *I shan't* (archaic in US English, colloquial in British English)

Ain't → *am not, is not, are not* (*ain't* is slang)

Many teachers and copy editors insist that no contractions should appear in formal prose. Using them sparingly seems to make sense. Again, though, this is a matter of style, not grammar.

Apostrophes for Pluralization

Sometimes, apostrophes indicate plural, such as when pluralizing initials or using the plural of letters:

👍 Both Puneet and Arpita had PhDs in English. [No apostrophe needed for abbreviations.]

👍 They both had straight A's in college.

👍 "Mind your p's and q's," was what Puneet's mother always told him, urging him to be attentive to matters of decorum.

Dates and numbers (1990s, fours, 8s and 9s) do not require an apostrophe.

Apostrophes and Possession

Apostrophes also indicate possession, which is often more difficult than it would at first seem. They can also indicate when something is an aspect or part of something, as in expressions like "earth's atmosphere" or "the dog's tail." Here is an example of a singular proper noun in the possessive form:

👍 Puneet's goal was to get to the bottom of the alien-invasion situation.

Joint possession uses just one apostrophe:

👍 Puneet and Arpita's hard work seemed to be drawing unwanted attention, though, particularly from people who simply wanted to destroy the alien invaders.

But these two hardworking journalists have different writing styles, and this next example sentence alludes to those two different styles. This is not a joint ownership situation:

👍 Puneet's and Arpita's writing styles differed quite a lot.

Noncountable nouns ending in *s*, like the names of diseases (*diabetes*, *measles*) or of fields of study (*classics*, *geophysics*, *acoustics*), and words like *scissors*, *tongs*, *tweezers*, *pants*, and many others also take *just the apostrophe* to indicate possession, as there is no difference between singular and plural forms.

👍 While physics' attraction was initially great, Puneet decided instead to major in English.

👍 Measles' ravages were evident on Puneet's skin, but Arpita was lucky to have had a much milder case.

Regular plural forms, which end in *s*, take just an apostrophe:

👍 Behind all of the domestic unrest, of course, was the aliens' continued presence.

In sum, to show possession of a plural noun (typically ending in *s*), just add an apostrophe: *the five friends' plans*, *the products' packaging*, *the Tagores' house.* If the plural form is irregular and does not end in *s*, you need to use an apostrophe + *s*: *the bacteria's virulence*, *the children's toys*, *your teeth's health.* (You might opt for *the health of your teeth* in that last example, though.)

Pronouns such as *its*, *his*, *hers*, *ours*, *yours*, *theirs* all end in *s*, but they do not take an apostrophe. *It's*, which some have cited as the most frequent wrong word usage in English, is not the possessive form of *it*! *It's* is a contraction for *it is* or *it has*. The possessive of *it* is *its*. Verbs ending in *s* do not require an apostrophe, either: *wants*, *likes*, *writes*.

Double Possessives

People often wonder about the situation where we have an "*of*-phrase," which signifies possession and also something after it which seems to call for an apostrophe:

👍 Selina was a friend of Puneet's. [This is called the "double possessive."]

👍 Selina was a friend of Puneet.

Both of these forms are acceptable. Traditionally, only the second sentence was acceptable. The double possessive seemed to be perhaps redundant. But the double possessive makes sense in sentences like this.[3]

Where Does a Possessive Apostrophe Go?

Here is how to determine where to place an apostrophe. Let's take the sentence about Puneet and Arpita's combative neighbor, Garrastazu:

> 👎 👍? Garrastazu's guns were mounted on his living room walls.

Is the possessive form and its apostrophe correct here?

Here is a four-step process that you might use in order to determine placement of the possessive apostrophe.

1. First, figure out what the *nonpossessive form* of the proper noun would be. You can do this by modifying the sentence so that it does not require a possessive form, inserting an *of* or a *belonging to*.

   The guns *belonging to* Garrastazu were mounted on his living room walls. [This operation reveals that *Garrastazu* is the nonpossessive form.]

2. Now insert this nonpossessive form back into the original sentence. It won't indicate possession just yet, but gives us the base form of the proper noun, what's sometimes called the "uninflected form."

   Garrastazu guns were mounted on his living room walls.

---

3   Garner has some good examples of the double possessive construction and offers the compromise solution of restructuring a sentence with a double possessive. "Many colleagues of Dr. Siegel's" he turns into "Many of Dr. Siegel's colleagues" (713). He calls the double possessive a "Stage 5 rule," something that is generally "adopted except by a few eccentrics" (Roman numeral page l). In short, a double possessive is OK for almost everyone.

3. The next step is to determine whether the proper noun is singular or plural and whether it ends in *s*, *z*, or neither. With this knowledge in mind,

—For nouns ending in *z* or *s*,

- If it is singular, add an apostrophe + *s*. [This is not the case here, as the name does not end in *z* or *s*. If the name were *Jones*, then you would have *Jones's*; in the case of *Gomez*, the form would be *Gomez's*.]

- If it is plural, add only an apostrophe. [Again, not the case; *Garrastazu* is singular. If we were talking about his family, as in a sentence such as "All of the *Garrastazus* guns were mounted on their living room walls," then we would have *Garrastazus'*.]

—For all nouns ending in a letter other than *z* or *s*,

- Add an apostrophe + *s*, regardless of whether it is plural or singular. [The case with our example: *Garrastazu's*.]

4. Insert that word back into the original sentence:

👍 Garrastazu's guns were mounted on his living room walls.

Some styles, such as the Associated Press (AP), require only an apostrophe after a name that ends in *s* or *z*: *Jones'*, *Gomez'*.

A small number of words that are not really possessives used to be seen as requiring an apostrophe: *for goodness' sake*, *for conscience' sake*, *for righteousness' sake*. These apostrophes are being dropped now in most writing, even the most formal, though you'll still see them from time to time.

Ellipses

Ellipses are three dots, which indicate one of two things. Either you are suggesting a pause of some kind in your writing . . . or you have quoted something and are omitting some words from the quotation. If you end a full sentence on an ellipsis, you will have to add a fourth dot. . . . And keep in mind that if you quote and use ellipses, you want to honestly convey the idea of the original. If a professor's recommendation reads, "In class, he was excessively voluble, talking all the time, drowning out his fellow students, and he rarely did good work outside of class," you shouldn't add ellipses to convert this to "In class, he was . . . voluble . . . and he . . . did good work outside of class." This is a dishonest modification of the original. But this kind of thing happened to my words once when I was quoted in a local college's newspaper. The takeaway? Don't be dishonest when you modify a quotation. And be cautious about what media outlets you grant interviews to.

10

A Special Case

COMMAS

Commas cause no end of headaches. Part of the problem is that people have long been given poor or conflicting advice about commas: "Commas indicate pauses"; "Commas are basically optional"; "Comma use is just random." Such declarations are not very helpful. Commas do indicate pauses, but other marks of punctuation do so as well. Some commas are indeed optional; most are not. And some people write good English using a lot of commas, while others write good English using commas quite sparingly.

So you see, commas are a bit problematic. I think it's useful to conceptualize commas as having four basic functions: to set off or separate added information; to set off or separate a sentence element for special emphasis; to indicate a pause and/or to clarify meaning; or, conventionally, which is to say in a way codified by longstanding use. Table 3 summarizes these four basic functions of commas.

Table 3. Uses of the Comma

Importance	Use			
	To set off added information.	To set off elements for special emphasis	To indicate a pause and/or to clarify meaning.	"Conventional" uses.
Very important and necessary; can be confusing if omitted.	Joining two or more main clauses with coordinating conjunction.	To set off introductory elements. To indicate contrast or emphasis, for example in a "tag question" ("You understand, don't you?").	To separate items in a series (especially if last two can be misread as an appositive), and with coordinate adjectives: X, Y, and Z. (This usage is sometimes called the "serial comma" or "Oxford comma.")	With dates, degrees, and addresses: "As of October 29, 2017, Arpita Tagore, PhD, lives at 121 Ontario Avenue, Pequa, NY 10025." To show direct address; use after salutation in informal letter: "Dear John, . . ." When representing dialogue: "Arpita said, 'I am very tired now.'"
Somewhat less important, but still usually necessary to convey intended meaning and to prevent confusion.	Joining very short main clauses with coordinating conjunction. Use with nonrestrictive appositives. Use with other nonrestrictive elements.	To set off introductory element of fewer than four words. To set off "interruptives" like *however*, *though*, *on the other hand*.	Natural pause. After a Subordinate clause. Used to mark omission of a verb: "She was tired; he, perky."	∅
Not exactly optional, but getting there.	∅	Use with mild opening interjections: "Well," "So," or "Right."	N.B.: Some styles (AP, *New York Times*) prohibit/discourage use of serial comma.	∅

Commas Used to Set Off
Added Information

Commas sometimes serve the simple function of allowing you to add material to a sentence, to increase the specificity of what you're saying, or to link ideas more tightly to each other than they would be if you used two separate sentences.

Commas Used to Join Two or More Main Clauses

Remember that a main clause is, quite simply, a sentence. You can join it to another main clause (that is, another full sentence that can stand on its own), by simply adding a comma and a coordinating conjunction (one of the ABSOFNY words), which I highlight below:

- Most of the populace was gradually coming to accept the invasion, *but* anti-alien fringe groups were militantly opposed to the visitors.

- Puneet and Arpita interviewed as many people as they could, *and* they converted these interviews to published articles.

- The CIA agent who had visited them had not returned, *so* they were starting to feel safe from persecution.

However, note that when the main clauses are short, the comma is optional.

- Their nights passed slowly. Arpita worried *and* Puneet snored. [Since the second sentence contains such short main clauses, no comma is needed.]

Commas Used with Nonrestrictive Appositives

Restrictive modifiers (appositives or adjective phrases, usually) are not set off with commas. These modifiers limit the meaning of a noun and are therefore absolutely necessary or required in order to convey that word's meaning. Sometimes they are called *essential* rather than *restrictive*. I have an example earlier concerning Garrastazu's dislike of nosy newspaper reporters (page 42). An everyday example I like is "The landlord hated students who were messy," where "who were messy" is needed—is restrictive, essential for the meaning. The landlord hated *only the messy* students.

When you want to introduce a nonrestrictive element, though, commas are used. If you write, "The landlord hated students, who were messy," the meaning is that the landlord actually hated *all students*. The "who were messy" is only additional information not required to convey the main idea (even though it might give a reason the landlord hated students). It's only an add-on to your sentence's core meaning.

Here is a sentence with a nonrestrictive appositive:

👍 Our president, Mr. Akbaliatuk, seemed only to be making matters worse.

Note that within the world of this narrative, Mr. Akbaliatuk is the president, a fact that is well-known to the characters in the story. Thus the proper noun that appears as an appositive—*Mr. Akbaliatuk*—is not really necessary to include in order to convey the sentence's meaning. Everyone knows that he is the president, and the information can be dropped with no loss of meaning. Putting commas around it signals that fact.

Here is another nonrestrictive appositive:

👍 Puneet and Arpita, the town's reporting duo, had come under federal scrutiny.

Puneet and Arpita is more or less equivalent to *the town's reporting duo*, and in this narrative, they are the only reporting duo in Pequa, so you use commas to indicate it's just repetition of known information.

By contrast, sometimes an appositive is restrictive, essential for communicating the sentence's meaning:

👍 Puneet's friend Selina was also a reporter.

Puneet's friend is in apposition to *Selina*, but since Puneet presumably has more than one friend, the appositive (*Selina*) is necessary information and should not be separated with commas. The name Selina indicates which friend, exactly, the sentence is talking about. You need that name in there to convey your meaning. By contrast, setting it off with commas would suggest that Puneet had only one friend. Perhaps that would be the case if Puneet were a sociopath or if he were deserted on some island with only Selina for company. But that's not the situation here.

You have to determine if a repeated noun element of your sentence is absolutely necessary for conveying your meaning (is restrictive or essential), or if it's just giving some rewording of previously mentioned information (is nonrestrictive or nonessential). If it's restrictive, no commas are needed. If it's nonrestrictive, use commas.

Commas Used with Other Nonrestrictive or Nonessential Elements

The following sentences provide additional examples of nonrestrictive elements set off with commas. Again, these are set off because they are *not really necessary* to the meaning of the sentences. I have boldfaced the nonrestrictive elements:

👍 The aliens, **who had invaded people's households**, were all small, no larger than a couple of feet across.

The words in bold indicate extra information that is not necessary to the meaning of the sentence. The sentence notes that aliens had invaded everyone's household, but the important information conveyed—that is, the point of the sentence—is that *all* of the aliens were small in size. The additional, background material is set off with commas. Contrast this:

👍 The aliens who had invaded people's households were all small, no larger than a couple of feet across.

In this comma-free version, the same relative clause is restrictive or essential, as it's attempting to distinguish what is special about just those aliens that went into people's houses: they were small ones, though the sentence hints that larger ones might be out and about. (Later on, we will see that there are some "outdoor aliens.")

Let me offer one more example of a nonessential clause set off with commas:

👍 A heavily armed citizenry, **attempting to destroy the invaders**, ended up damaging property or injuring innocent bystanders.

In this last example, the participial phrase (*attempting . . .*) is a nonrestrictive modifier and set off with commas. It's only added information and not essential to the sentence's meaning. Without the commas, the meaning would be about only that heavily armed segment of the citizenry that was attempting to destroy the invaders. With the commas, the sentence describes the entire citizenry.

Commas Used to Set Off Elements for Special Emphasis

Although elements set off by commas are sometimes unimportant (nonessential to the meaning), in some situations commas can accentuate and foreground the elements that they precede or follow.

Commas Used to Set Off Long Introductory Elements

A "long introductory element" is typically at least four words, though there's no universally agreed-upon rule about the number. If you would like to emphasize the importance of your sentence opener, you may use a comma after a shorter group, even after a single word:

👍 Then, something even more extraordinary happened.

👍 After a few weeks, people came to realize that something changed in themselves when they came into contact with the alien puddles.

👍 Amid nationwide near-panic, people began to question their prior beliefs.

Commas Used to Indicate a Contrast

Since they have the effect of setting off information, commas are often used to emphasize something that contrasts sharply with antecedent material in a sentence:

- 👍 People soon began loving, not fearing or hating, the aliens. [Em-dashes could, alternatively, be used here to set off "not fearing or hating."]

- 👍 Dipping their hands into the alien puddles calmed, maybe even tranquilized, humans. Some thought that was the way the aliens would take over the planet, but there did not seem to be any attempt to take property or anything else. The aliens just passively existed. [*Calmed* and *tranquilized* are not quite opposites, but represent stages of relaxation.]

Tag questions, which I discuss earlier, in the section on comma splices (page 53), also fit into this category:

- 👍 "We don't really know what's going on, *do we*?" Arpita asked her husband.

- 👍 "I'm actually not sure of anything anymore, are you?" Puneet replied.

Commas Used with "Interruptives"

An "interruptive" breaks the flow of a sentence, as if the writer or speaker were interrupting themself and offering a contrast. Words that serve this function include *though*, *however*, *on the other hand*, *by contrast*, or a similar subordinator or conjunctive adverb:

- 👍 She wanted, *though*, to understand.

👍 Puneet realized, *however*, that as a species humans were far from any significant communication with the aliens. [You might optionally place commas after *that* and *species*. They are not necessary, but putting them in would highlight the set-off phrase *as a species*.]

Commas Used with Mild Interjections

Use a comma after a "mild interjection" *hey, well, so, then, darn, oh*.

👍 "Hey, Arpita, maybe we should simultaneously dip our hands into the aliens? I've heard that this doesn't affect them but offers a calming feeling—or something."

👍 "Well, I'm still a little afraid to touch them myself," Arpita said, "much less to dip my hands in them."

Commas Used to Show a Pause and/or to Clarify Meaning

All comma usages indicate a certain slight pause. Here are some more details in determining what sort of pause requires a comma.

Commas Used to Separate Items in a Series (Oxford or Serial Comma)

When you have a series or a list of some kind (*x, y, and z*), many people have been taught that you need to have a comma after each item including the last one, the one just before the conjunction. This comma is commonly known as the Oxford or serial comma. It causes considerable controversy since journalists do not use it. It is also not used in British English, nor even by Oxford University Press! Critics of the Oxford comma see it as pretentious and unnecessary. I recommend its use unless you are writing in a style where it's prohibited. My take on the Oxford comma is pragmatic: it never weakens your expression to include it, and it's sometimes confusing to omit it. For example, in 2017, the absence of an Oxford comma in the wording of legal guidelines cost a dairy company five million dollars (see Victor).

You need to be careful, however, not to use a comma when you have an appositive set up:

👍 If the two intrepid journalists, Puneet and Arpita, were confused about the alien situation, then many of their readers likely would be as well.

👎 If the two intrepid journalists, Puneet, and Arpita, were confused about the alien situation, then many of their readers likely would be as well. [This makes it sound as if we are talking about four people here—two intrepid journalists as well as Puneet and Arpita.]

I'm not sure why the Oxford comma generates so much controversy. Here are some more examples:

👍 It wasn't the time, place, or occasion for people to take to the streets.

👍 In fact, Puneet and Arpita spent more time indoors than ever, did more work, and felt better about themselves than they ever had.

👎 Puneet said he owed it all to his parents, the puddle alien and Arpita.

In the last sentence, which omits the Oxford comma, the sentence evokes an absurd universe, one in which Puneet's parents are the puddle alien and Arpita. As the judge in the Maine case wrote, "For want of a comma, we have this case" (Willingham).

You will need to check which style guidelines your writing needs to abide by. (If you are writing for a newspaper, avoid the Oxford comma unless you have another career option readily available.)

Commas Used to Indicate a Natural Pause

What's natural for some is not natural for others, but sometimes the only guideline that makes sense is that when reading the sentence or saying it aloud, there's a definite pause:

- 👍 Simultaneous group contact with the aliens seemed to result in a very weird experience, at least initially.

- 👍 It was as if the alien puddles brought people closer together, creating in the humans something akin to telepathic communication with one another. [If a phrase at the end of a sentence starts with a present participle ("creating"), you generally have a pause that requires a comma.]

Commas Used after a Subordinate Clause

When you start a sentence with a subordinate clause, you should follow that clause with a comma prior to the introduction of the main clause, *but* if the subordinate clause comes after the main clause, the comma is usually dropped:

- 👍 Although Puneet and Arpita were supposed to be objective and unbiased, they had formed an emotional connection with the alien in their own home. They were not sure why.

🏳 Things had changed so much, because everyone was frazzled by the invasion of only a few weeks ago. [No comma needed.]

🏳 👍 Most people felt fairly hopeful, although they were not sure what would happen in the near or distant future. [In this case a comma works, perhaps because the second clause reverses or challenges the meaning of the first. I would use it but don't see it as absolutely necessary here.]

If you start with the main clause and add a subordinate clause, as in two previous example sentences, try it out with and without a comma. Sometimes there's enough of a pause to warrant a comma even though the general practice is to not use a comma in this situation.

Commas Used to Mark an Omission

Sometimes a comma will replace an *and* or a *then.* At other times, it can replace more words:

👍 Their neighbor would shout, then curse, when talking about the invading aliens. [First comma replaces an *and.*]

👍 Many citizens loved the puddles' aesthetic beauty; others, the puddles' companionship; and still others, the way the puddles brought them together with family or friends. [The verbs (probably *loved*) in the second and third clauses are left out and replaced with commas.]

Uses of Commas That Have Become Acceptable by Virtue of Convention

Commas used in these situations increase the clarity of the material being presented by separating key elements. Also, these usages are simple, and readers expect to see commas in these situations.

Commas Used with Dates, Degrees, and Addresses

👍 Puneet Tagore, PhD, lived at 121 Ontario Avenue, Pequa, NY 10025.

👍 On December 8, 2033, the world changed forever.

Commas Used When Indicating Direct Address and after Salutation in Informal Letter/E-Mail

"Direct address" is when something written or said is directed to an individual, as in the following:

👍 "Arpita, are you happy?"

👍 "Darling, I've never been happier!"

Letters might begin and end in the following way:

👍 *Dear Arpita,*

The situation is changing rapidly. International stuff. Message me about your whereabouts and let's meet up to work out a plan.

Love,
Puneet

Commas Used When Representing Dialogue

If you are writing fiction, or if you need to introduce a quotation in a sentence, a comma is needed:

👍 When they met, Puneet said, "Something very weird is going on. I am not sure what to make of it."

👍 "Neither am I," Arpita agreed.

Comma use is difficult but, I think, ultimately manageable. Work on it. When you punctuate carefully, your prose gains exactitude and persuasiveness. You are able to say more precisely what you mean because the cues given by punctuation lead your reader in the right direction. As I have suggested earlier, a lot of punctuation involves making a personal choice, some options meaning one thing, others meaning quite something else.

PART SIX
Comprehensibility

One significant factor in getting across your idea and message is, quite simply, what words you choose. Does your audience understand your every word? Are you confusing your audience by using metaphors and other rhetorical devices that seem to be either inappropriate or at odds with one another? Does your writing include informalities (slang or jargon, for example) that some audiences would find either off-putting or simply incomprehensible? And are you using the right word, not one that sort of approximates the right word but actually isn't? This part of *Stellar English* will look at some word-level issues that have the potential to devalue your message—or to embolden and empower it.

11

Creating Understandable Sentences

METAPHORIC LANGUAGE, PARALLELISM, JARGON, SLANG, AND CLICHÉS

What Is a Metaphor?

Whether your sentences and ideas are understandable often hinges on how well you use figurative language, such as metaphors. Note that even in the previous sentence I have inserted a metaphor with my use of *hinges*. In their influential book *Metaphors We Live By*, George Lakoff and Mark Johnson write that "human *thought processes* are largely metaphorical" (6), and they then go on to explore how metaphors fundamentally help us shape and make sense of the world. Not surprisingly, our language overflows with metaphors. The challenge is controlling them—keeping them from overrunning their banks and flooding nearby towns.

Mixed Metaphors

It's fine to use an occasional elaborate or improbable metaphor, but you need to make sure that you stay consistent within the verbal universe your metaphor is helping to establish. To put

A **metaphor** is a comparison of some kind, sometimes including *like* or *as* (including these makes for a particular kind of metaphor known as a *simile*). We often make comparisons and bring in ideas or images apparently unrelated to the issue at hand but which shed light on what we're discussing in a special or striking way. For example, one might say of a good science fiction movie, "I felt as if I'd entered a dimension of non-carbon-based entities," or as Ralph Waldo Emerson said of a famous person who is never challenged, "Whilst he sits on the cushion of advantages, he goes to sleep" (298). Such expressions tend toward the poetic, but there are more everyday ones, too. In his novel *Cassidy's Girl*, David Goodis writes about the Port of Philadelphia: "The big ships rocked on the black water like monstrous hens, fat and complacent in their roosts" (22). And this way of using language is by no means recent. In the ninth-century epic poem *Beowulf*, the narrator describes someone about to speak, "The leader of the troop unlocked his word-hoard" (848).

it another way, your metaphors should not offer opposing figurative expressions, as the following all do:

- 👍 🗨The TV pundit said, "Admittedly, we're trying to recover. But the rebuild needs some good bones before putting up any wallpaper." [This gets a thumbs-up only because it's a quotation. In fact, the quoted passage is a mixed metaphor.]

- 🗨 Though it caused a ton of problems, the alien invasion created a fast track for international cooperation. ["Ton" and "fast track" don't work together.]

👎 Sometimes the cookie crumbles jelly-side up; other times it falls flat on its face. [This includes three metaphors, all at odds with one another.]

👎 Garrastazu proudly held a machine gun. He patted it and said, "This is my baby, a real peacekeeper." ["Baby" is at odds with "peacekeeper."]

And here is one, slightly modified, from Toby Fulwiler and Alan R. Hayakawa's *Pocket Reference for Writers* (47):

👎 "We must fight against the tide of cynicism that threatens to cloud our vision," President Akbaliatuk declared. [Akbaliatuk might opt for a more consistent metaphor: "*swim* against the tide of cynicism that threatens to *drown our reason*" would be preferable.]

Most mixed metaphors are, ultimately, understandable, but they might make your reader pause, briefly imagine the absurd universe that they summon up, laugh, and then move on. During that brief period of processing, some meaning gets lost.

Parallel Constructions

English sentences work by setting up various patterns. As I explain in chapter 1, for example, most sentences start with a subject (a noun phrase) or include their subject near the beginning of the sentence. Sentences must have verbs, and those verbs must be tensed (again, must indicate when an action or state is taking place). There are often repeating elements to sentences: lists, for example, or adjectives modifying some other element, or even repeated main clauses.

While I have mentioned all of this before, I have not emphasized that when your writing includes some repeated elements, you need to make sure that each instance of repetition is substitutable with any other. They all have to take a similar form. For example, here is a sentence that sets up an adjective-use pattern but then departs from it:

☞ The populace was divided, angry, ill-informed, no one wanted to communicate, and threatened. [The third element should be *noncommunicative*.]

The first two of this next group of examples set up a pattern of infinitive use:

☞ They wanted to work together, to overcome the crisis, coming out in a better state, and to triumph. [The third element should be *to come out in a better state*.]

☞ To run, to hide, to fight, and strategizing what to do next were the initial responses. [Three infinitives in a row need to be followed with another infinitive, not a participial.]

☞ To run, hide, fight, and strategize what to do next were the initial responses. [Note that in this parallelism of infinitives the *to* may be dropped after the first one. But using the *to* all four times would also be OK.]

Reason is . . . because constructions also fall into this category. Saying *the reason is* implies *because*. Using *because* indicates the speaker or writer has forgotten about their *the reason is* construction:

☞ The *reason* the populace was so divided with respect to the alien invasion *is because* some people saw positive benefits to the puddle people—they were pleasant companions, entities that somehow induced calmness—while others just resisted and rejected change of all kinds. [Should be *the reason is . . . that.*]

👎 The *reason* that guns were being confiscated is *because* there were just too many of them, and many people were wildly shooting at the aliens and creating collateral damage of untold magnitude. Trouble is, the *reason* Akbaliatuk was elected was *because* he was such a gun lover. [Should both be *the reason is . . . that.* In the second instance, though, *because* may be omitted.]

I am sad to say, however, that my battle against *reason is . . . because* constructions is likely a losing one. The expression has made its way into the language and is here to stay, I fear. Still, careful writers and speakers will continue to avoid its use. I hope.

Jargon and Slang

Often, you will use a word that you think is perfectly acceptable, but it's not formal English; it's slang. The nineteenth-century British novelist George Eliot (yclept Mary Ann Evans) offers an interesting idea about slang, though. She writes in *Middlemarch*, "I beg your pardon: correct English is the slang of prigs who write history and essays. And the strongest slang of all is the slang of poets" (quoted in Pinney n.p.). Eliot's point is that slang is a type of language intended for an extremely specific audience and often not fully accessible to the general populace. It can be the "slang of poets" or of "prigs who write history and essays," or it can be the slang understandable to people who live in a particular region, or who are of a particular ethnicity, say, or who have similar jobs or professions, or who share hobbies and enthusiasms. It might include unusual or archaic words, like *yclept*, which means *also known as*.

It seems to me that Eliot is talking about jargon, not slang, though the two concepts blur slightly. Here is some more jargon: If I were to write, "I just rode my 531DB LeChamp, which is first-gen full Campy N.R. with tubies, drillium calipers, and a Brooks pro,"[1] you wouldn't know what I was talking about unless you were as much of a bicycle enthusiast as I am—and about the same age. Language is intended to communicate, and jargon communicates with only a sector of the populace.

How do you know that the words you use might not be acceptable to an audience? This seems to me a basic question that few writers have bothered to ask or answer. The answer is simple: your words are not acceptable and your message might not get across if either the usage is too informal for a general audience—or if, when addressing a specialized audience, you fail to use their language. In both cases, you need to learn how to code-switch: you need to adopt the version of English understandable to most of the people in your audience. Thus if you address a general audience, you'll need to code-switch into formal English. When addressing specialists, enthusiasts—that is, a homogeneous group—you should code-switch into the English that they typically employ. With that specialist audience, using jargon confirms your status as an insider.

---

[1]   This means "I just rode my bicycle, which is made of double-butted Reynolds 531 steel tubing and is equipped with Campagnolo parts from the early 1970s, including brakes that have had holes drilled in them for lightness, as well as with tubular tires and a Brooks Professional saddle." Trouble is, even this elaboration won't make all that much sense to someone not an old roadie.

Slightly alarmingly, some "business-speak" words have spilled over from specialist audience jargon into everyday speech. Words like *impactful*, *liaise*, *deliverable*, *drill down*, *bandwidth*, *operationalize*, *skillification* seem to come up all too often. Here is one I recently heard:

👎 He was efforting to understand the situation. [*Trying* is preferable to *efforting*, which is not in fact a word.]

If and when these usages become part of ordinary discourse, they are acceptable to use for general audiences. Many have not just yet. Garner has a "verbal change" scale that categorizes words that are "Stage 1," used by a "small minority," but normally considered "outright mistakes." On the other end of the continuum, there is the "Stage 5" usage, which he labels "a linguistic fait accompli" (l), which is to say that the change has happened. It seems to me that you need to make a decision in every writing situation: what is it that your audience expects? Is this an audience that will only accept "Stage 5" language? Will it put up with less than conventionally acceptable wording? Perhaps the point is that language is always changing and adapting to a changing world, so that if we stick with totally conventional usages, our language will lag behind what's going on. As my earlier example of Coleridge's disdain for a certain usage might suggest (page 117), we need to be more accepting, finally, of innovations and changes imported from specialist audiences. (But sorry, I can't accept *efforting*.)

Unlike jargon, much slang will be completely understandable across multiple groups. I mean, I can readily process words like *ain't*, *whazzup*, *no biggie*, *cool it*, *buzzed*, *strung out*, *whacked*, *woke*, and even *LOL*, *tbd*, *YOLO*, *SMH*, *ROTFL*, and much vulgar slang. But when these words or initialisms are used in the middle of a formal essay or presentation, it's jarring, even unnerving. Then, too, these words are understandable only up to a point. There's a vagueness, an ambiguity, a fuzziness surrounding slang words that we're all familiar with. What exactly is a *no biggie*? What does the sociologist Erving Goffman mean in his essay entitled "Cooling the Mark Out"?[2] How inebriated is *buzzed*? (I want a blood alcohol level.) If you are striving for exactitude, slang is not your best option.

Slang also includes certain sentence constructions, such as,

👉 👇 "I ain't got no time for no aliens," Puneet's neighbor said. [Slang. "I don't have time for aliens" or "I have no time for aliens" would be preferable. The sentence is OK insofar as it's a quotation, though.]

This example sentence is a double negative, or actually a multiple negative, and it's obviously not formal English.

Interestingly, such constructions have found their way into academic writing, and seem to be acceptable there:

👉 👇 Puneet was not unhappy about the situation. [Better to say "he was happy" with it, though there is a slight difference of meaning.]

Other examples of more or less acceptable double negatives are expressions like *not unlikely*, *not unusual*, *not indifferent*, *not unexpected*. The prolific writer Derek Haines has a good short article on the issue, and he quotes the *Cambridge*

---

2   This means something like attempting to calm down and mollify the sucker who has just been duped or conned.

Dictionary to offer some guidelines for the use of double negatives:

> We can use not + an adjective or adverb with a negative prefix (for example, un-, in-) as a way of softening or downtoning the meaning of the adjective. The meaning becomes affirmative, but the double negation shows that the writer/speaker is cautious about it.

Still, though, and Haines and I are in agreement here, you should be cautious when attempting a double negative in formal writing.

The Cliché

I also suggest that you be alert for any clichés that have found their way into your writing. They tend to diminish the impact of writing and speech. These are usually figurative expressions that have flooded popular discourse. Often they derive from a line in a Shakespeare play or from the Bible—or from some historical event that almost no one remembers. But they have been repeated so frequently, and by so many people, that they have little or no rhetorical impact.

If someone says, "There's something rotten in the State of Denmark," they are quoting *Hamlet*, but the language has become tired and dull through multiple uses. Similarly, if I say, "I march to the beat of a different drummer," most people will think, "Heard that before," even though the expression, first penned by Henry David Thoreau, once had originality and power. By contrast, if I quote Shakespeare's *Julius Caesar*, "Cowards die many times before their deaths; the valiant never taste of death but once," I'm using lines from the Bard that most people have not heard often, so it's not (or not yet) a cliché. (It's also slightly hard to understand.).

Keep in mind that when you use a cliché, it obscures rather than clarifies meaning. It diminishes comprehensibility. If you say a baseball player "runs like a deer," what exactly does that mean? Fast? Loping? Quickly accelerating? Thirty-one feet a second? (A deer can run about fifty-eight feet per second. No human has ever approached that speed—so the simile is actually ridiculous.) It's just a trite expression of an idea and gives us no real insight into or special angle on a player's ability to run the bases. It just means that a player is fleet of foot. Sports announcing traffics heavily in trite expressions and clichés, though occasionally some striking metaphor or expression will emerge.

What is the test of whether something is a cliché or not? It's simple. If you have heard the figurative expression at least fifty million times (give or take), it's a cliché. But if it floats your boat, go for broke, hit the streets, take it to the limit, and knock yourself out. There are five: if you Google "cliché," you can find lists of hundreds of others. But beware: you'll be opening a can of worms.

12

Word-Level Issues

A Note on Spelling

English spelling can be quite confusing and even illogical at times. Many words are simply not pronounced the way that they're spelled: *light, through, minuscule, though. Otiose* (pronounced *o-she-ose*), and *victuals* (pronounced *vit-ls*) are two of my favorites. And while I could certainly reproduce here a list of difficult-to-spell words, such a list would not be all that useful since everyone has their own spelling demons. I recommend that you keep a small dictionary, look up words that you have trouble spelling, and make a check mark in the margin of the dictionary next to every word you look up. You might review your checked words from time to time, just in order to firm up their correct spellings in your mind.

But a few points to consider include the following. Make sure that you spell proper nouns correctly. Get the names right! This issue is vital because many names are spelled in improbable ways (look at my last name, for example). Once I asked a former colleague for a letter of recommendation for tenure, and she agreed, in fact sending me a copy of what she wrote. She started off by spelling my last name correctly, but about halfway through, *Cioffi* became *Coffi*, and in her last paragraph I was referred to as *Frank Coffee*.

I expect that autocorrect was to blame for these misspellings. Autocorrect will often silently and swiftly modify words according to some algorithm. It can be helpful, correcting my *thier* to *their* instantaneously, but its correction of names is less valuable. What you need to do, in a step that my colleague evidently skipped, is simple: proofread your writing. If you are writing an important letter, make sure that you spell the names correctly. If you are writing about literature, the characters' names are all in the text you're discussing, so reproducing them accurately shouldn't be a problem. Misspelling proper nouns suggests you couldn't be bothered with such trifles. But my advice is to take the time to get them right. Not doing so diminishes your audience's confidence in you.

American versus British English

US English and British English are remarkably close, but some usages and spellings differ. While I cannot list all the differences here, my suggestion is to be consistent within a single piece of writing: if you write *colour* and *fibre* in one place, continue on with those British spellings throughout. The key is to keep in mind who you are writing for. If your work is to appear in a British publication, use British spellings; if it will be in an American one, stick with spellings like *color* and *fiber*, and avoid words like *boot* and *bonnet* when referring to the trunk and hood of a car.

Sometimes it's hard to distinguish the two variants. *Flavour* and *behaviour* are British spellings of *flavor* and *behavior*, but *contour* is spelled the same way on both sides of the Atlantic. *Metre*, *fibre*, and *litre* are British spellings, but *timbre*, *spectre*, and *theatre* are both British and American. If you were taught British English and are now writing for an American audience, or vice versa, you need to consult a list of words that have different spellings/meanings in the two English varieties, at least before you finalize (or finalise) your work.

Sometimes, too, British and US English differ on other matters: for example, in British English, corporations or companies are always considered plural entities (British: "Omega are now part of the Swatch group"). (I recommend Nelson's discussion of British versus US English [188–90]. He is particularly good on this since, being based in Hong Kong, he likely had to deal with both variants.)

Confused Words

There are many books that list confused words and that explain how to choose the best one for a given meaning. I have relied on Bremner, Dreyer, and Garner, as well as on multiple dictionaries, both British and American. What I offer here is only a tiny fraction of the difficult and/or confused words in English. These are the ones that, in my experience, seem to cause writers the most anguish.

Fifty Problem Words

affect / effect

Affect is typically a verb:

👍 The world was, on the whole, significantly *affected* by the invasion.

Affect also appears as a noun, though not all that often. It means *emotionality*.

👍 Whenever Puneet went to talk to his next-door neighbor, Garrastazu, it always ended up a high-*affect* situation.

By contrast, *effect* is usually a noun. It means *result*.

👍 The *effect* of Puneet's visits to Garrastazu was, to this point, negligible.

Just to make things difficult, *effect* can also be a verb, meaning *to cause*.

👍 In order to *effect* change, though, Puneet felt he had to still make the attempt to reason with Garrastazu—and with a surprisingly large percentage of the populace.

alot

Alot is not a word. *A lot* means *many* or *much*. It is slightly informal, but acceptable in formal English. A *lot* (noun) is a piece of property or a group of objects for sale, perhaps at an auction.

amount / number

Remember noncountable nouns and countable nouns? *Amount* refers to noncountable nouns, while *number* refers to countable nouns. A large *amount of love*, a *huge number of problems*. *Less* and *fewer* are similar, with *less* referring to noncountable nouns and *fewer* to countable nouns. When you see "Ten items or *fewer*" in your grocery store, you know you have a grammarian somewhere in the house. (Usually the signs say, "Ten items or *less*," though most people in the checkout aisle never abide by the number anyway, so what's the difference? The difference is that you still want to get the wording right.)

cite / site / sight

Cite is a verb meaning "to refer to or mention." *Site* is a locale—for example, the *site* of a crime (or a web*site*). *Sight* refers to something seen or to one's *eyesight*.

👍 Seen from satellite camera, it was not a pretty *sight*: in Eurasia millions of people were being herded into detainment camps, no one knew why.

👍 Tiananmen Square, the *site* of a national tragedy, was now being used as a gathering place for protestors.

👍 "I could *cite* a hundred articles on human response to major changes of various kinds," Puneet said, "and in general people resist change, even if it's for the better."

complement / compliment

Complement means *to match* or to *coordinate well with*. By contrast, a *compliment* is a positive statement made to someone. "His colorful tie *complemented* his shirt, and he received many *compliments* on the fashion choice." (You probably have also noticed the grammar term *complement*, which I use earlier several times.)

👍 It was an indirect *compliment* to the American people that they were allowed to stay in their homes. To some extent, the authorities trusted and respected the populace.

👍 Interestingly, the shimmering puddles of alien essence *complemented* most people's interior décor.

👍 No *complement* could fully express the feelings of most Americans. They were afraid. They were tired. They were uncertain. They were intrepid. They were confused. [The sentences starting with *They* all contain *subject complements of the adjectival variety,* and rename or describe the subject.[1]]

conscience / conscious / consciousness

These words are easily confused because they sound so much alike, and the differences in meaning are subtle. *Conscious* means awake and alert, or, more metaphorically, aware of something. *Conscience* is the part of the mind, intellect, or personality that informs you as to whether you're doing the morally correct or incorrect thing. You've probably heard of a "guilty conscience"—that is, one that is tugging at some portion of your brain and saying, "That would be wrong." *Consciousness* is a synonym for awareness.

- 👍 Puneet and Arpita were *conscious*, though, of an undercurrent of fear that had suffused their lives.

- 👎 "My *conscience* bothers me," Puneet confessed to his wife. "I think I should be doing more, more than just reporting and writing."

- 👎 Most people had only a very dim *consciousness* of how otherworldly these aliens really were.

continual / continuous

Continual suggests something that is happening repeatedly, while *continuous* implies that something is ongoing, like a flowing stream or river.

---

[1]   I discuss complements on page 97.

👍 Even though guns were outlawed, the sound of gunshots at night was *continual*.

👍 The *continuous* stream of online information kept people enMeshed for hours on end, till their eyes went bleary and their hands cramped.

discrete / discreet

Discrete means separate, all by itself. *Discreet* means something quite different—namely, the quality of being cautious, low key, and even a little guarded in reference to some action or thing. People talk about *discreet* packaging, say, of medical products sent in the mail; or of being in a restaurant and making a *discreet* suggestion to a dining partner that they have a piece of spinach caught in their teeth.

👍 There were three *discrete* responses apparent in the American public: acceptance, rejection, and total indifference.

👍 Puneet made *discreet* inquiries in his neighborhood in an effort to determine the status of the aliens housed nearby; he realized that this knowledge might be crucial for survival.

do / due

Do is a form of the infinitive verb *to do* (I *do*, you *do*, he/she/it *does*, we *do*, you *do*, they *do*). It means to act, accomplish, or accept. "'I *do*,' was Puneet's answer during the marriage ceremony" when he was asked, "*Do* you accept this woman to be your wife?"

Due is the adjective meaning *payable* ("your mortgage is *due* the first of every month") or *owing* ("*Due* to unforeseen circumstances, the college will be closed").

👍 He and Arpita would *do* what they could to inform their neighbors of the truth.

👍 *Due* to his diligence, Puneet was becoming almost famous as a pundit and writer.

I should note that some writers contend that *due to* should be avoided except when used adjectivally ("attributable to"), as in, "His thinness was *due to* his strict diet." Others suggest that careful writers should eliminate the expression altogether. If you find yourself using this expression, reread your sentence and try to figure out if there is a more direct way of expressing the same idea, but without the *due to*. If there is not, then you can keep that expression in place. There usually is, however: "His thinness was the result of his strict diet." "His strict diet had caused him to become thin."

hanged / hung

Most people don't realize that *hanged* is the past tense of *to hang (by the neck)* and just use *hung*, which is the past tense of the verb *to hang (something)*, such as a picture, a sign, or something else, but not a human.

👍 In some countries, people who were perceived to be cooperating with the invaders were publicly *hanged*. No one was cooperating with the aliens, so the *hangings* were cruel and pointless. Actually, all *hangings* are.

👍 On their wall *hung* a framed quotation from Ralph Waldo Emerson: "OUR STRENGTH GROWS OUT OF OUR WEAKNESS" (298).

imminent / immanent / eminent

Imminent means *about to take place*. *Immanent* means *intrinsic, inherent,* or *indwelling*. *Eminent* means *significant, important,* or *famous*.

👍 A world-ending disaster seemed *imminent*. The Eurasian dictator now claimed that the aliens were actually invaders from the West, beings created in US labs.

👍 *Immanent* in the American people was a fundamental goodness, a fundamental sense of decency, Puneet thought. He hoped there would be enough of that to save them.

👍 The most *eminent* commentators had nothing insightful to say about the issue, other than accept the aliens for what they were—totally benign beings.

imply / infer

These words are often confused. *Imply* means to subtly suggest, without directly saying something. *Infer* is what a reader or listener concludes about something or reads into something that's not explicitly stated.

👍 One of Puneet's articles seemed to *imply* to readers that they should actually dip their hands into the aliens: this provided a strange but wonderful sense of calmness and relaxation.

👍 Some *inferred*, though, that people should gather and together dip their hands into their resident alien. This inference was not something Puneet had intended, but it changed the world quite utterly.

its / it's

Its is the possessive of *it*. *It's* means *it is* or *it has*. I know I've mentioned this earlier, but it bears repeating, as the confusion between these two words is quite common.

👍 When two people simultaneously placed their hands in an alien puddle, there was a telepathic connection. "*It's* not clear what's going on," Puneet said when he tried this, "but I like it."

👍 When a group dipped their hands into a puddle, *its* influence was such that something beyond telepathy was established—a kind of communality that went beyond words.

lay / lie / lie

To lay means *to set* or *to place*. You might *lay the table* before a meal, or you might *lay* your pen aside in favor of a pencil when doing a crossword puzzle. *To lie* means *to fib, to tell an untruth*. Another meaning for *to lie* is *to lie down*. These verbs are all conjugated differently, as one might expect, and one form, the past participle of *to lie down*, is *lain*, which probably sounds strange to your ears.

Note that the common expression that is used to mean *to sunbathe*—namely, *to lay out in the sun*—should be *to lie out in the sun*.

Lay versus Lie

Verb	Present	Past	Present Participle	Past Participle
To lay (or set)	lay	laid	laying	(has/had/have) laid
To lie (down)	lie	lay	lying	(has/had/have) lain
To lie (fib)	lie	lied	lying	(has/had/have) lied

👍 At first, people would just *lay* their hands atop the alien puddle.

👍 When Puneet first read about this development, he needed to *lie* down.

👍 He hadn't *lain* down for five minutes when there was a knock at the door. Puneet answered. It was his neighbor Garrastazu, who shouted, "This whole thing is all a *lie*!"

led / lead

Led is the past tense of *to lead*: *I led the way, you led the way,* and so on (present tense is spelled *lead*, but is pronounced with a long *e*—that is, the same way that the letter *e* is pronounced). *Lead*, pronounced the same way as *led*, is the heavy metal, symbol *Pb*, atomic number 82. It is found in old plumbing, old paint, and most dark chocolate. It's poisonous.

👍 "Right," said Puneet. "That's what people told Moses when he *led* them to the promised land."

👍 Garrastazu didn't hesitate. "And guess who couldn't get in, who turned to a pillar of *lead*?"

👍 Puneet replied, "Look, you need to get your Bible references straight. You're talking about Lot's wife, who was turned into a pillar of salt, not *lead*. She was leaving Sodom and Gomorrah. I don't want to *lead* you astray, Garrastazu, but these aliens are harmless, maybe even helpful."

like / as

Like introduces nouns or noun phrases, while *as* introduces clauses.

👍 *Like* all journalists, Arpita and Puneet were curious. They located a group of close friends and family and initiated a group interaction with an alien.

👍 "*As* I wrote in my article last week," Puneet informed the gathering, "there is something nearly transcendent when we do this together."

👎 "*Like* I was saying, we need to be patient and observant." [Should be *As I was saying.*]

Like has also come to be used as a filler word. Using the word in this manner is, *like*, a mark of immature speech, *like*, an indication of informality, and *like*, a real annoyance to listen to.

loose / lose

Loose is an adjective meaning *not tight*, *inexact*, *shaky*, or even, in a slang usage, *wanton* or *secret-sharing*. *Lose* is a verb meaning *to not win* or *to not be aware of the presence of*. There are many expressions involving both of these words, which sound somewhat alike but carry different, though slightly related, meanings:

👍 Not wanting to *lose* sight of his objective, Puneet kept his pen and pad nearby to record his thoughts on the experience.

👍 Trouble is, the battery cover for his light/fan unit was *loose*, and the batteries fell out somewhere in the house. He didn't have time to look for them now, so he just set the device aside.

👍 "Loose lips sink ships," his professors had always warned him, but Puneet never figured out how that applied to reporters. Until now.

principal / principle

Principal, which is an adjective, has an "a" in it, which links it to its part of speech. It means *major* or *primary*. It's also a noun, meaning the *principal administrator* of a school (with the word *administrator* being dropped). In addition, *principal* is the word used in reference to investment, namely the amount of money that earns interest, or the *principal* (or major) actors in a play or film.

By contrast, a *principle* is a *rule*. (How to remember this? Both end in -*le*.)

👍 "The *principal* reason we are getting together today is to verify for ourselves what exactly this experience is like. So when we're done, let's just segue into a party!"

👍 The *principle* was scientific: hypothesize, test the hypothesis, and then modify it as needs be.

👍 Arpita's high school *principal* would approve; he was a big fan of empiricism.

then / than

Then means *next* or *presently*. *Than* is a comparative word meaning *in relation to* or *in comparison with*.

👍 *Then*, all ten people dipped their hands into the alien puddle.

👍 It was a lot better *than* partying, they realized; it was totally cerebral, transportive, and bizarre.

there / their / they're

These are all pronounced the same way, which makes them especially difficult. *There* is a word used to specify locale ("*There* he is!") or to offer a category ("*There* are five types of people"). *They're* is the contracted form of *they are*. *Their*, the possessive form of *they*, violates the "*i* before *e*" rule[2]:

👍 *There* was a knock at the door. Puneet got up. It was Garrastazu again. "Where is everyone?" he growled. "*They're* in the other room," Puneet replied. Maybe you would like to join them?"

👍 Garrastazu went in and saw the group with *their* hands immersed in the alien. His first impulse was to flee in horror, but when he saw the ecstatic expressions on people's faces, he bethought himself.

---

[2]   Many words violate this "*i* before *e* rule." The rule is just fine, except when your "feisty foreign neighbors, Keith and his wife, receive eight counterfeit beige sleighs from their friends, the caffeinated, atheist weightlifters. Weird."

too / to / two

Too indicates excessiveness, as in *too much*. (The extra *o* might be seen as excessive.) It also carries the meaning of *besides* or *extremely*. *To* is a preposition with many meanings, usually ones implying directionality. *To* also functions as part of the infinitive form of verbs. *Two* is the spelled-out numeral 2.

👍 "This is just *too* weird for me," Garrastazu said.

👍 "It's not, really," said Puneet. "It's not *too* bad. Give it a try, Garrastazu. Open yourself *to* new experiences. Try *to* let go a little. Hey, and what's your first name, anyway?"

👍 "I have *two* names, actually, my real name and what most people call me. My real name is Koldobika. But I ask people *to* just call me Louie."

whose / who's

Whose is a pronoun meaning the person or thing to which something belongs. It is also used as an adjective, as in "Whose woods these are I think I know" (Frost, "Stopping by Woods on a Snowy Evening" [207]). *Who's* is the contracted form of *who is*.

👍 It was not clear *whose* decision it was, but Garrastazu did join the group. In fact, all over the world, people had discovered what Puneet and Arpita and their friends had discovered: doing this as a group added a surreal but very pleasant dimension to their lives.

👍 At some point, over the course of time, about a dozen world leaders got together and performed a similar ritual. Something very strange happened. *Who's* to say what the explanation was? But the leaders suddenly saw eye to eye, seeing the world simultaneously from their own perspective and from that of eleven others.

All Fifty Words in an Extended Example (👍)

The *number* of theories about what finally *effected* the departure of the alien puddle people was all but overwhelming. When the first group of a dozen leaders had jointly immersed their hands in an alien, many of their close friends and family were indirectly *affected*. The leaders had changed, possibly mellowed. But it was not enough; not enough of the *eminences* across the entire world had taken part in the process.

The idea was to find a large enough alien puddle to accommodate some two hundred world leaders, the leaders of all the countries on earth (along with a few leaders of countries that are unrecognized as such). Many large alien puddle people were not residing within people's houses. In Pequa, New York, a cave housed an enormous alien puddle person, and per-haps because the local reporters Puneet and Arpita Tagore had gained fame for their reporting on the invasion, that cave was chosen as the *site* of the alien encounter with the world's leaders. Puneet and Arpita were allowed to cover the event, provided they did not use their nail-mon recorders or videos.

The *amount* of hype surrounding this happening was palpable, as its *effect* on our planet was likely to be inestimable. People were aware of *imminent* catastrophe or *imminent* salvation of some sort. Who would be *affected*? Maybe everyone, but *a lot* of the enthusiasm was merely curiosity about what was going to happen next.

It was quite a *sight* in Pequa. The leaders had been brought *there* in *their* respective limousines—the brands and models too numerous to *cite*. The fashionable and expensive clothing they wore *complemented* one another's. When they first arrived, in fact, nothing but polite *compliments* were exchanged. Outside the cave in which the huge alien puddle person had settled, a river flowed, its roar *continuous*, forming a background auditory soundscape. There was *continual* flashing of nail-mons cameras.

Puneet and Arpita were *conscious* of the gravity of the event, but they also had a *consciousness* of just how fortunate they were, as local reporters from Pequa, to enter the cave with the world leaders and witness firsthand what was happening. Puneet knew that he wasn't supposed to take photos inside the cave (only the leaders were allowed to do that), but he set up a video recording on his nail-mons, and with a clear *conscience*. This event was *too* important not to be recorded. He would be *discreet* about it, but he had to have this on record.

Due to the language difficulties, the leaders soon formed into *discrete* groups, mostly defined by continent of origin. Versions of English were what they all spoke with one another, which was convenient for Puneet and Arpita. They didn't want to get *hanged* because they didn't understand an important statement. *Like* most reporters, they valued accuracy.

On the walls of the cave *hung* ivy and, somewhat frighteningly, bats. The huge alien puddle person glimmered and glistened. *Its* odd half-light was *immanent.* It at once basked in it and seemed to produce it. Two hundred yards across, it could have been mistaken for an underground lake.

It *lay* undisturbed, its surface as uniform and smooth as a sheet of ice. Many of the leaders walked around it; some *lay* down to rest until the immersion began, and as the crowd quieted, a seriousness emerged.

The American president, Qarqangaarjuk Akbaliatuk, *led* off. "I won't *lie* to you," he said. "This is scary but I think necessary." With that, he kicked off his shoes, stepped into the pool, and was soon swallowed up by it.

Amazingly, the others followed his *lead.*

Puneet and Arpita watched, aghast, stunned. It was *as* if their limbs had turned to *lead.* Puneet *loosened* his tie and said, "I guess we should join them—I mean, what do we have to *lose?*"

Arpita replied, "No, wait. Are you crazy? Our *principal* job is to record what happens. And we need to see what *they're* experiencing. Don't forget that."

"But diving into a liquid alien with the two hundred most powerful people in the world—we probably won't have that chance again. And to witness what they are experiencing, we have to be in there, don't you think?"

Arpita considered the idea. "I'll pass," she said. "You've got to remember. We're writers. Writers. *Who's* to say what's going to happen here? We're observers and reporters *whose* job it is to just record what happens." She paused. "But do what you want—" She broke off.

The leaders continued to enter the pool, some less eagerly than others.

Puneet said, "One of us can observe from the outside, but the other has to experience what the world leaders are going through. That would be me. I guess."

Arpita nodded. She at first didn't know what to say. Then she said, "Shouldn't that be, 'That would be I?'"

"Nope," said Puneet. "Subject case follows only after a conjugated form of the *to be* verb."

"You've been doing some research," Arpita shot back. Then she paused. "Oh, btw, what are the pass-words for your computer and e-mail?"

Puneet laughed. "You're *implying* I won't survive. Don't worry," he said. "I'll be back." He walked slowly toward the alien puddle, turned at the last moment, and waved to Arpita. Her eyes shone. She waved weakly.

The president of New Zealand was entering the pool at the same time. Puneet said, "After you, President."

She replied, smiling, "No, no, you go ahead."

Within a space of five minutes, Puneet and all the leaders were swallowed up by the alien puddle. *Then* Arpita was alone, alone in a cave with a huge, glowing, iridescent pool. Bats on the walls made scary, chirping noises. Arpita enMeshed and started dictating:

"This is Arpita Tagore, reporting for the *Pequa Post-Dispatch*, from a cave somewhere in upstate New York.

"I have just witnessed what must be one of the most extraordinary events in the history of humanity. Over two hundred leaders from all over the globe assembled in this cave and gathered around a huge alien puddle person that looks like a small lake. After exchanging pleasantries with *their* counterparts, they then proceeded to wade or dive into what looks like a silvery, shimmering pool of water. Within less than five minutes, they all disappeared beneath the surface. Along with the leaders, my husband, the intrepid reporter Puneet Tagore, went in as well. The pool's surface is once again mirror smooth."

She disenMeshed. Then, to calm herself, she did five or six of her favorite yoga poses—downward facing dog, warrior, half-moon pose, triangle pose, tree pose. The *principle* she followed was the same as always: get the pose exactly right, and then hold it perfectly for sixty seconds. Longer than that would be *too* long.

Close to half an hour passed. Then Arpita saw some disturbance on the pool's surface, and the world leaders began to come out.

Arpita enMeshed to resume her story. "The world leaders are now emerging one by one from the huge puddle. President Akbaliatuk has surfaced and from here, looks more beatific *than* alarmed, more knowing *than* confused. They all seem to have aged, though, this reporter notes. The president of Finland has gray hair, even though she is only thirty-two. The dictator of Eurasia, long known for his spryness, is being assisted by the ruler of the newly formed Talibanistan."

When Puneet came out, Arpita swiftly disenMeshed and ran to him, hugging him tightly. "You made it!" she said. He too had aged. She could only *infer* that he had been through a lot.

Later, no one knew exactly *whose* expression it was that captured the day's event, but one of the leaders' remarks was recorded and *then* enshrined in newsfeeds all over the world: "It was raw, completely honest communication that sustained us for three decades of life inside the strange, alien world. We were all of us on the same page. We could speak and convey our ideas fully. We shared—no, it was far more *than* that—we inhabited . . . a universal grammar."

PART SEVEN
Consequentiality

I have been claiming here that knowing and using formal English can improve your chances of success at creating a piece of writing that has your intended impact. Again, it's not the only or even necessarily the best language, but it's an extremely useful one, and often the most effective at conveying your ideas to a given audience. To be able to employ formal, correct English easily and seamlessly can prove exceptionally valuable. The inverse certainly holds true, too: not having mastery of and fluency in this variant of English might handicap you in important situations. People judge you by your language use—all too often, negatively.

Despite this reality, which I think would be accepted by most readers, many people have little idea of how to construct an English sentence. Many, like Xinyi, whom I have not forgotten, have no idea whatsoever of what a "flying comma" (that is, an apostrophe) does on the page. A large number of people have only a very hazy notion, in fact, of what a sentence is. Grammar and punctuation are just not taught that much anymore. In a kind of passive, clumsy, but de facto cooperation, our culture—including many educators—

undervalues knowledge of how to put together clear, effective, forceful sentences. People who teach this skill are low-paid and overworked. Examples of poor English multiply and proliferate.

I have heard the argument that formal grammar such as the one I present here is racist, classist, and maybe even sexist. I disagree. Those who want to simply throw out the whole enterprise of sharing the basics of formal written English are only courting chaos and silently endorsing a status quo. Their suggestions, I fear, represent sanctimonious bad faith. Formal English grammar should be available to anyone who wants it, regardless of race, gender, ethnicity, or national origin.

It might be that many people don't get the necessary preparation in this subject because rhetorical power and eloquence—competence in formal written English—provides an extraordinary power, maybe too much power. People who can control and skillfully employ the fundamentals of language and rhetoric might have other things to do than noodle around on the Internet or spend hours on Instagram, or for that matter spend a lot of time shopping online or hanging out at the mall. Having an influential, articulate voice is the first step toward challenging the status quo.

~

Most people hope their writing will have the capacity to make a difference in the world. Using the grammar and usage I have suggested will not by itself assure this. You need more. You need to have good ideas. You need to look for places in your subject area where things just don't seem to add up, don't really align with your experience, intuitions, or convictions.

That's the start: find places where something is confusing or worrisome and needs to be made sense of. You then need to read what others have said about the issue. At this point, you might share your ideas with trustworthy and supportive—but honest—others. Think *tough love*. You need to write and rewrite. Then, rewrite some more. Writing isn't simply easy (or hard) work; it's continuous effort often made in face of possible disaster, of the disaster that the world might be spiraling into, of personal disaster of many kinds, and of the disaster that no one will care about what you've written or will even bother to read it.[1]

What I'm saying is this: consequentiality is a significant challenge, a difficult goal, but knowing grammar and usage will help you to achieve it. Here are a few ways that your grammar and usage will help you create writing that matters.

First, if you closely attend to issues of grammar and usage, your writing will not stigmatize you. It will have credibility just by virtue of its form, its confident use of language, its precise punctuation, its avoidance of the trite and expected. It won't be easily dismissible by an audience. Your *ethos*, the version of your *self* that your words project, will be a positive, effectual, trustworthy one.

Second, your language, grammar, and usage might allow you admittance to an ever-changing but important group of serious people—namely, one willing to genuinely engage your ideas and evaluate their importance, validity, and impact. Do you want to join and be taken seriously by some group of professionals that uses formal written English and that does

---

[1]   I discuss these multiple writing strategies in more detail in my book *The Imaginative Argument: A Practical Manifesto for Writers.*

almost everything it can to prevent new "members" from joining? Well, first off, to get in, you need to speak their language. And once you're admitted, you might try to lessen their snootiness even as you embrace their strict standards for communicativeness and accuracy.

My third point is a suggestion. When your writing doesn't seem to convey anything like what you want, it will often be because the language you're using is vague, ambiguous, confusing, or ungrammatical. But don't give up. To get more of a there there, explore the language and punctuation you're using. This often leads to a greater understanding of your subject. Working on your grammar subtly forces you into a deeper investigation of your ideas, each modification of your language giving you time to consider and reconsider the content of your message. If you focus on your grammar and your manner of expression, if you try out various phrasings and re-phrasings, you'll see that, like our narrative's puddle people—creatures that can assume a variety of physical forms—your ideas too can change their shape. You then can decide which shape is best for your intended audience.

Remember, though, no matter how complex your subject matter is, you should still work to express your ideas about it in as lucid and as grammatically accurate a way as possible. When your words say what you want them to say and do so without the distraction, without the stigma of grammatical errors, of slang, of jargon, of unclear sentence structures, or of irregular punctuation, you dramatically increase the chances of communicating to others your ideas about the most challenging issues and puzzles of your topic, your discipline, and, finally, of our world—and maybe even of our universe.

Epilogue

Puneet slipped his feet into his old shoes. They felt a bit loose, but they'd conformed so well to the shape of his feet that it didn't matter.

"So," Arpita said. "What was it like in there?" Then, "Hey, your hair's gone gray!?"

"Right," Puneet answered. "We were there a long time; a long, long time. I don't know where to begin telling you what happened."

"A long time? How long do you think were you in that alien pool or puddle or whatever, honey?"

"About thirty years," he said. "Give or take. Time is of course highly subjective."

"You must be joking," Arpita said. "You were gone, like, half an hour."

Puneet could read her look as her eyes drifted up to take in his hair, his receding hairline, and then slowly refocus on his deeply seamed face. "They told us that we'd probably de-age once we got back to our own dimension," he said. "But I'm not sure how long that will take."

"'They'? Who are 'they'? And 'probably' de-age?"

Puneet laughed. "Sorry. Pronoun antecedent error." He paused. "The 'they' refers to the Guardians, the

Watchers, the Originators—not sure how it should be translated. You know, the puddle people people."

"What? The 'Originators'?" She shook her head. "What did they look like? More puddles? Did you get a photo?"

"They were nonphotographable, I'm afraid," Puneet replied. "Not puddles, though kind of puddlesque. Non-Euclidean."

Arpita gasped, shook her head, looked at her suddenly elderly husband. Then after a short pause, she asked, "What did you do there, then? How did you spend those thirty years, while I just hung out here, enMeshed off and on, did a few asanas, and listened to the horrid bats?"

"Hey, sorry to keep you waiting! Remember, I suggested we go in together." He didn't want to sound as though he was scolding, so he added, "But it's good that you were here, recording what went on for the rest of the world to see."

He paused for Arpita to respond, but she let him continue. "Well, I got to know the world leaders very well, you might say. I mean, I lived almost half a lifetime there with them in Zhu-Oh-Tekap. An amazing group."

Arpita shook her head. "I don't get it. What's in the pool? Was it really another dimension or something? Zhu-Oh—what? Another world? Is that it?"

"It was a world, for sure, sort of a Shangri-La, really. Zhu-Oh-Tekap. You remember that novel by James Hilton, *Lost Horizon*?" Puneet tied his shoes. "People were kidnapped and brought to this idyllic, wonderful hidden valley in Tibet or something. Well, we weren't kidnapped, but we found a Shangri-La of sorts—a utopic world of peace, of calmness, of studying and reading. Libraries, parks, mountains, everything. This pool, this huge alien puddle person"—he gestured toward it—"Look, it's getting smaller now!"

They both stared at the shrinking puddle person.

He sighed, shook his head, and went on. "The pool was a portal, I guess, but at the same time, a presence. We were fed, housed, clothed, pampered. There were beings from other planets, from other galaxies there too. Some humanoid, some not. Some truly not. Really not." He paused, shook his head, then looked at his wife. She was so beautiful he didn't know where to look at her. "I really missed you!"

Arpita and Puneet hugged again, almost convulsively.

"How did you and the others leave, then?"

"Well, we learned that a window, an opening in the portal, happened once every thirty years. The earth contingent all voted to come back en masse the next time it opened. I guess they felt an obligation to improve or make some impact on the planet. Or something." He locked his eyes with Arpita's. "I just wanted to be with you again."

"A great decision!" Arpita said. They kissed again, this time longer, more deeply.

～

Arpita combed her hair into place with her fingers. She said, "So, what did you do there, there in that alternate world?"

Puneet stared into the gradually accumulating darkness. "I spent most of my time reading and writing. In fact, most of us did. Writing was our main activity, weirdly enough."

Arpita nodded. "I guess that's not too surprising. What did you write?"

"A lot. Maybe twenty books. We've come out with a whole library among us."

"C'mon! Where are those books now?"

He sat up. "Right here, of course," he said, enMeshing and projecting a document. "We all shared what we wrote in Zhu-Oh-Tekap."

Arpita laughed, shook her head. This was all so unbelievable. She enMeshed. "The aliens are all disappearing, world-wide. Amazing." She tilted her hands toward Puneet, so the 3-D news announcer was visible to him too.

After her hands starting tiring, Arpita disEnmeshed and asked, "So, what did you write about?"

"My experiences. Your experiences. Some novels and plays. The one I've been working on for the past couple of years has been a book on English grammar."

"*English grammar?* Really? Why?"

"Because the others wanted me to. I wasn't a head of state, and I was the only professional writer, so—" He paused, looking at Arpita.

"But you're not even a native speaker," she pointed out.

"Yeah, I think they saw that as an advantage. And I'm basically a native speaker since I came over at age four."

"True, true," Arpita replied.

"English was the only shared language among the earth contingent, and there were varying degrees of fluency."

The cave was now almost completely dark. Reclining on a smooth, relatively comfortable rock, Puneet went on. "So grammar lessons and a book were needed, I realized—or I had somehow been instructed or influenced to think this. At any rate, the world leaders got into it. Here's a sentence I tantalized them with. It has eight words that look all the same, but some are adjectives, some verbs, and some nouns: 'Buffalo buffalo buffalo Buffalo buffalo Buffalo buffalo buffalo.' It's correct English. I recalled it from a college linguistics course. They loved that kind of thing."

Arpita rolled her eyes. "Goofy." Then, "What does it mean?"

"'Buffalo' is the name of a city, it's what a bison might be called, and it is a verb meaning 'to bully' or 'to confuse.' So the sentence means something like 'Buffalo bison bully Buffalo bison [that other] Buffalo bison bully.'"

Arpita hesitated. "OK. I guess, 'Syntax trumps morphology,' is the lesson." They both flicked on their nail-mons flashlights and stood up. "Look!" Arpita said. She shone her nail-mons flashlight toward where the huge alien puddle person had been. It had by now completely disappeared. "Incredible," she said.

She lay back down on the large rock. "But wait," she said after a minute or two, "didn't you say they all had access to libraries of books and so on?"

"Yes, but they really wanted a book from me." He paused. "And—I hope this is OK—its main characters are named Puneet and Arpita."

"Us?" She thought for a few seconds and then said, "Well, why not? So it's a memoir-slash-grammar handbook. How wild is that!? Did your friends, colleagues, whatever, like it?"

"I haven't quite finished it, actually, so no one's seen it."

Arpita paused. "Amazing. Amazing."

"I still don't have a title for the book," Puneet confessed. It felt so good to be back with Arpita that he could hardly stand it. "Any suggestions?"

They got up and started walking out of the cave. Their nail-mons flashlights illuminated a path. Arpita thought for a few moments, then laughed and gestured toward the ceiling of the cave. "How about this," she said, pausing. "'Stellar English'?"

Puneet looked at her to see if she was joking. "Well, OK, in the sense that 'stellar' means super-good or something?"

"Right," Arpita said. "That's part of it. But also looking at language is sort of like looking at the stars; when words align in certain ways, you can glean meaning from them—you know, through clear and compelling sentences—the same way you can envision constellations, or for that matter, other worlds, other galaxies, when you look at the stars."

Puneet nodded slowly. "I like it," he said. "Yes, I like it."

Arpita smiled. They made their way toward daylight. "So how did your grammar book start out? What was your 'hook,' as we call it?"

"Well," said Puneet, "it starts out in a kind of basic way." He stopped walking. "Quote, 'This grammar handbook relies on the truth of the proverbial expression from Caius Titus, *verba volant, scripta manent*: spoken words fly off, written ones remain.' End quote."

Arpita stopped and didn't say anything for about fifteen seconds, but then said, "Latin? C'mon. Surely we can do better than that!"

Arpita started walking again.

"But that's the idea behind all these books about grammar and writing!" Puneet protested, following Arpita's path.

"Yeah, yeah, sure. But no, that won't do," she said, not turning around to speak. "The expression just means 'get it in writing.' Let's see," she said. "It's a book for the world leaders. Hmm. They're not really writers, most of them, but they're ambitious and smart I guess . . . most of them have been through a lot—and probably don't want some quote from Caius Titus or whoever it was. Give me a minute."

Arpita thought a few seconds, as she noticed how pungent the air was at the mouth of the cave, how eerie the continuous squeaking and chirping of the bats behind them. She and Puneet were almost out in the open by now.

Arpita said, "How about something like this?" She looked at the cave's opening to the outside world.

"I'm waiting," said Puneet.

They both stepped into the open air. The bright sunlight made them squint.

She turned to her husband and said, "OK, here you go: 'Writing matters.'"

For Further Reading

TEN INDISPENSABLE RESOURCES

This book is just a brief overview of grammar. If you want a "full-scale" grammar book, I strongly recommend Rodney Huddleston and Geoffrey K. Pullum's superlative *The Cambridge Grammar of the English Language* (2002), or the slightly less recent but still extremely authoritative volume, *A Comprehensive Grammar of the English Language* (1985) by Randolph Quirk and Sidney Greenbaum, et al. These nearly 2,000-page books are indeed comprehensive. A shorter (900-page!) excellent grammar guide is *The Grammar Book* by Marianne Celce-Murcia and Diane Larsen-Freeman. Though intended for English language teachers, it also offers valuable insights for non-teachers.

All three of these books, however, would take the average reader months to work through, and ideally, that reader should be simultaneously taking a graduate-level linguistics course taught by someone who can guide them in this detailed, rigorous, and difficult subject. Just the same, having those books in your library is valuable insofar as they provide ready reference on just about any issue of grammar that concerns you.

Less demanding but still very comprehensive grammars include *Understanding English Grammar* by Martha Kolln, Loretta Gray, and Joseph Salvatore; *English: An Essential Grammar* by Gerald Nelson; and *Grammar: A Pocket Guide* by Susan J. Behrens. Focusing more on style than exclusively on grammar, *Artful Sentences* by Virginia Tufte and *Dreyer's English* by Benjamin Dreyer are also extremely valuable books whose scope far exceeds this volume's. These five books, accessible to the average reader, helpfully explain many of the complexities of English grammar and usage that I lack the space to deal with in detail here.

If you are a real usage nerd, though, Bryan A. Garner's *Garner's Modern English Usage* is the one to buy, to consult often, and to rely on for sober, useful advice. This volume is one that my wife and I go to again and again every week. It's not only valuable for its many insights about usage, its myriad examples, and its comprehensiveness. It's also accessible and understandable to the average person. It's also, at times, hilarious.

I also recommend *The American Heritage Dictionary of the English Language*, 5th edition. Weighing in on matters of style, meaning, and usage, this dictionary's "Usage Panel" of about two hundred experts rules on what they consider correct and appropriate uses of words and expressions in English. The experts come from a variety of fields and often disagree with one another. But that's OK. That's partly why their suggestions are so valuable.

Acknowledgments

I have dedicated this book to the memory of my twin brother, Grant, who taught literacy education for close to three decades at the University of New Hampshire. After his death, I met his students and colleagues, and they were as shattered by his untimely demise as they were unanimous in their praise for him and his teaching. He inspired and taught so many to be better readers or better teachers of reading. For me, for many others, the world broke apart with his death. It will never be the same.

~

I want to gratefully acknowledge and thank my longtime editor at Princeton University Press, Peter Dougherty. I also want to thank Matt Rohal, of Princeton University Press, who took over the editing of this book after Peter retired. Matt was unfailingly patient and professional. He offered careful line edits and honest, insightful responses to my work, and he encouraged me to persist with a project that sometimes seemed to me both frustrating and overwhelming. I count myself very fortunate that it was he who took over this project.

Sara Lerner did a wonderfully efficient job of moving this book through its many stages, one of which was finding Jennifer Harris, my copyeditor, to copyedit it. Jennifer was consistently thorough and precise as she genuinely engaged the perplexities of grammar as well as my own occasionally idiosyncratic interpretations and weird English. In addition, she was sensitive to all the complexities of the book's layout. Many thanks to you both.

The six anonymous reviewers of my book proposal, the four anonymous reviewers of the manuscript, and the six Princeton University faculty members on the PUP Editorial board all also deserve thanks, as these scholars' careful reading and prudent commentary helped me shape this book into a more coherent whole.

On the country's opposite coast, in Washington, Joseph Powell was a great virtual companion over these pandemic years. He has helped me get through a very difficult time, while we co-authored our "Coronajournal," which documents and describes our own and our world's travails. His careful, poetic prose, his attention to detail, and his unflinching honesty served as a model for me.

Beata Williamson, a professor at the University of Gdańsk, buoyed and heartened me from across the pond, and she helped clarify a number of issues regarding how nonnative speakers of English conceptualize the often confusing and difficult grammar of our language.

Many thanks also to David Thurn and Carol Cook. Yoga instructors with doctorates in English, they helped me calm my soul, as they offered regular insights into language, literature, and the body-mind-spirit connection.

I also want to extend my gratitude to Chris Poon and Mike Tweedle, whose enthusiasm for this book's scope and encouragement for its narrative line were much appreciated, and who helped me through the often arduous task of writing.

Thank you to Arpita Kohli and Puneet Girdhar, chocolatiers of distinction, who allowed me to use their first names for my main characters of this book's narrative, and who offered me insights into Hinduism.

Baruch College–City University of New York generously granted me fellowship leaves that allowed me to finish this book, and I want to extend my thanks to those faculty members and administrators who so kindly supported my work. I also want to acknowledge and thank my students at the college, especially those who took my grammar courses and writing courses.

My Baruch English department colleagues helped me get through what's been an exceedingly difficult time for us all. Tim Aubry, Jessica Lang, and Corey Mead deserve especial thanks, as their advice and encouragement were instrumental in helping me complete this project. Vince DiGirolamo, in the history department, with whom I team-taught a seminar on the Italian American narrative, also has been both an exceptionally supportive and helpful colleague and fellow union activist.

Carole Allamand, a Swiss professor of French at Rutgers, and my bike riding companion for decades, patiently listened to my long disquisitions on English grammar and was a willing though sometimes captive audience for my ideas about this book. A critic, a language teacher, and a novelist, Carole was the ideal person to consult about this book's strange multi-genre character.

I want to extend an especial and colossal thanks to my colleague Gerry Dalgish, who worked intensively with me on the section about determiners, helping me clarify my own ideas and contributing extensively to part 4 ("Confidence"). Gerry is meticulous, incisive, and erudite—and at the same time, supportive and encouraging. This combination makes him a fabulous teacher and linguist as well as an extraordinary asset to the college. I deeply appreciate his guidance and help.

Ann Whitehill, William Cioffi, and Robert Cioffi have been steadfast family members whose support and love have never wavered.

Finally, my largest debt of gratitude goes to my wife and life partner, Kathleen M. Cioffi, a book editor and writer herself. She offered countless suggestions and ideas for this book, and (to cite a single small example) her counsel about hyphenation—and all matters of English grammar, not to mention design and layout—was utterly invaluable.

Works Cited

Adorno, T. W. *The Jargon of Authenticity*. Routledge, 2002.

Allcott, Lisa. "Reading On-screen vs. Reading in Print: What's the Difference for Learning?" *National Library*. 11 October 2021. https://natlib.govt.nz/blog/posts/reading-on-screen-vs-reading -in-print-whats-the-difference-for-learning.

Altreuter, Judith A., et al. *MLA Handbook*. 9th ed. Modern Language Association, 2021.

American Heritage Dictionary of the English Language. 5th ed. Houghton-Mifflin, 2011.

Armantrout, Rae. "Arch." *The New Yorker*, 12 September 2016, 68–69.

Aronson, Elliot, and Carol Tavris. *Mistakes Were Made (But Not by Me): Why We Justify Foolish Beliefs, Bad Decisions, and Hurtful Acts*. Brilliance Audio, 2014.

Baker, Russell. "How to Punctuate." https://docslib.org/How-To -Punctuate-By-Russell-Baker.

Baron, Dennis. "A Brief History of Singular 'They.'" *Oxford English Dictionary*. 4 September 2018. https://public.oed.com/blog/a -brief-history-of-singular-they/.

Barrett, Grant. *Perfect English Grammar: The Indispensable Guide to Excellent Writing and Speaking*. Zephyros, 2018.

Barshay, Jill. "Evidence Increases for Reading on Paper Instead of Screens." *The Hechinger Report*. 12 August 2019. https:// hechingerreport.org/evidence-increases-for-reading-on-paper -instead-of-screens/.

Baumgartner, Michelle, et al. "20 Must-Visit Websites to Learn English Online." *FluentU: English Language and Culture Blog*.

https://www.fluentu.com/blog/english/learn-english-grammar
-online/.

Behrens, Susan J. *Grammar: A Pocket Guide.* Routledge, 2010.

Beowulf. Translated by Seamus Heaney. *The Norton Anthology of World Literature,* vol. 1, shorter 4th ed., edited by Martin Puchner et al. Norton, 2019, pp. 842–912.

Bremner, John B. *Words on Words: A Dictionary for Writers and Others Who Care about Words.* Columbia UP, 1980.

Brunvand, Jan Harold. *Be Afraid, Be Very Afraid: The Book of Scary Urban Legends.* Norton, 2004.

Carson, Anne. *Autobiography of Red: A Novel in Verse.* Vintage, 1999.

Celce-Murcia, Marianne, and Diane Larsen-Freeman. *The Grammar Book: An ESL/EFL Teacher's Course.* 2nd ed. Heinle and Heinle, 1999.

Chicago Manual of Style. 15th ed. Chicago UP, 2003.

Chi'en, Evelyn Nien-Ming. *Weird English.* Harvard UP, 2004.

Cioffi, Frank L. *The Imaginative Argument: A Practical Manifesto for Writers.* 2nd ed. Princeton UP, 2018.

———. *One Day in the Life of the English Language: A Microcosmic Usage Handbook.* Princeton UP, 2015.

Coleridge, Samuel Taylor. *Specimens of the Table Talk of Samuel Taylor Coleridge.* https://www.gutenberg.org/ebooks/8489.

Conan Doyle, Sir Arthur. "A Scandal in Bohemia." *Sherlock Holmes: The Complete Short Stories.* John Murray, 1928, pp. 3–29.

Dalgish, Gerard M. "The Syntax and Semantics of the Morpheme *ni* in Kivunjo (Chaga)." *Studies in African Linguistics* 10, no. 1, 1979, pp. 47–63.

———. E-mail to the author. 16 August 2022.

Dreyer, Benjamin. *Dreyer's English: An Utterly Correct Guide to Grammar and Style.* Random House, 2019.

Eliot, George [Mary Ann Evans]. *Middlemarch.* https://www.gutenberg.org/files/145/145-h/145-h.htm.

Emerson, Ralph Waldo. "Compensation." *Essays and Lectures.* Library of America, 1983, pp. 283–92.

Empson, William. *Seven Types of Ambiguity.* 1930. Meridian, 1955.

The Fly. Directed by David Cronenberg. SLM Productions / Brooksfilms, 1986.

Frost, Robert. *Robert Frost: Collected Poems, Prose, & Plays*. Ed. Richard Poirier and Mark Richardson. Library of America, 1995.

Fulwiler, Toby, and Alan R. Hayakawa. *Pocket Reference for Writers*. 2nd ed. Pearson, 2005.

Garner, Bryan A. *Garner's Modern English Usage*. 4th ed. Oxford, 2019.

Goffman, Erving. "On Cooling the Mark Out: Some Aspects of Adaptation to Failure." *Psychiatry* 15, no. 4, 1952, pp. 451–63.

Goodis, David. *Cassidy's Girl*. Dell, 1951.

Haien, Jeannette, *The All of It*. Harper, 1987.

Haines, Derek. "Double Negatives in Writing Are Not Always a Mistake." *Just Publishing Advice*. https://justpublishingadvice.com/double-negatives/.

Hilton, James. *Lost Horizon*. Grosset & Dunlap, 1933.

Huddleston, Rodney, and Geoffrey K. Pullum. *The Cambridge Grammar of the English Language*. Cambridge University Press, 2002.

Jabr, Ferris. "The Reading Brain in the Digital Age: The Science of Paper vs. Screens." *Scientific American*. 11 April 2013. https://www.scientificamerican.com/article/reading-paper-screens/.

Kolln, Martha, et al. *Understanding English Grammar*. 10th ed. Pearson, 2016.

Lakoff, George, and Mark Johnson. *Metaphors We Live By*. U of Chicago P, 1980.

Lispector, Clarice. *A Breath of Life*. Translated by Johnny Lorenz. New Directions, 2012.

Macfarlane, Robert. *Landmarks*. Penguin, 2015.

Mayo Clinic. "Hiccups." https://www.mayoclinic.org/diseases-conditions/hiccups/symptoms-causes/syc-20352613.

Miller, D. O. "A Discourse Analysis of Clause-Final Multiple Adverbials." University of California, Los Angeles, MA thesis, 1991.

Munroe, Randall. *Thing Explainer: Complicated Stuff in Simple Words*. Houghton Mifflin Harcourt, 2015.

Nelson, Gerald. *English: An Essential Grammar*. 3rd ed. Routledge, 2019.

Nietzsche, Friedrich. *Twilight of the Idols*. Translated by Walter Kaufmann and R.J. Hollingdale. https://www.handprint.com/SC/NIE/GotDamer.html.

Ogden, C[harles] K[ay]. *The System of Basic English.* Harcourt, 1934.

Pinney, Thomas. *A Short Handbook and Style Sheet.* Harcourt, 1977.

Quirk, Stanley, and Sidney Greenbaum. *A Comprehensive Grammar of the English Language.* Longman, 1985.

Ross, John Robert. "The Category Squish: Endstation Hauptwort." *Papers from the Eighth Regional Meeting Chicago Linguistic Society, April 14–16, 1972.* Chicago Linguistic Society, pp. 316–18.

Shostak, Seth. "Drake Equation." Seti Institute. July 2021. https://www.seti.org/drake-equation-index.

Shteyngart, Gary. *Super Sad True Love Story.* Random House, 2010.

Tufte, Virginia. *Artful Sentences: Syntax as Style.* Graphics Press, 2006.

Victor, Daniel. "Maine Comma Dispute Is Settled as Drivers Get $5 Million." *The New York Times.* 9 February 2018. https://www.nytimes.com/2018/02/09/us/oxford-comma-maine.html.

Watson, Cecilia. *Semicolon: The Past, Present, and Future of a Misunderstood Mark.* Ecco, 2019.

"What Is a Comma Splice? With Examples." *Grammarly.* https://www.grammarly.com/blog/comma-splice/.

Willingham, A. J. "An Oxford Comma Changed This Court Case Completely." *CNN Health.* 16 March 2017. https://www.cnn.com/2017/03/15/health/oxford-comma-maine-court-case-trnd/index.html.

Index